CM0074086B

THE
STUDIO

A PSYCHOANALYTIC LEGACY

with love

C...u~

(Christina , 2015)

Gill Gregory

First published in 2015 by
Free Publishing Limited

Copyright © 2015 Free Publishing Limited

The author's rights are fully asserted. The right of
Gill Gregory to be identified as the author of this work
has been asserted by her in accordance with the
Copyright, Designs and Patents Act 1988

A CIP Catalogue of this book is available from
the British Library

ISBN: 978-1-8534322-1-7

All rights reserved; no part of this publication may be
reproduced, stored in a retrieval system, or transmitted,
in any form or by any means, electronic, mechanical,
photocopying, recording or otherwise, without the prior
written permission of the publisher. Nor be circulated in
any form of binding or cover other than that in which it is
published and a similar condition including this condition
being imposed on the subsequent purchaser.

Typeset by
www.chandlerbookdesign.co.uk

Printed in Great Britain by
Berforts Information Press

BY THE SAME AUTHOR

NON-FICTION

The Sound of Turquoise

The Life & Work of Adelaide Procter

POETRY

In Slow Woods

FOR
my mother
Dinah Gregory
(1927 – 2014)

&

in memory of my father, Dr. Basil Gregory
and my brother, Andrew Gregory

To
Sally Kilmister
friend & gentle critic

CONTENTS

Acknowledgements

I would like to thank the following individuals and organisations for their encouragement, ideas and invaluable help in the genesis, research and writing of *The Studio*: Isobel Armstrong, Tricia Bickerton, Nicola Bion, Betty Bradbury & the late Laurence Bradbury, Nicholas Clark & Caroline Harding at the Britten-Pears Library, Simone Coxall, Agnes Cserhati at Rufus Books, Robin Dettre at The Smithsonian, Stephen Duffy, Dulwich Picture Gallery, Elizabeth Jane, Lucy & Robert Gregory, Nicholas, Annabel & Marian Gregory, Mario Guarnieri, Joanne Halford at The Institute of Psychoanalysis, Sally Kilmister, Laura Marcus, Noreen McGuire, Andrew Motion, National Gallery, Leonee Ormond, Harriet Parks, Jesus & Nuria Puig, Christina Pehlivanos, Deryn Rees-Jones, Andrew & Isa Roberts, Boika Sokolova, Frances Spalding, Prints & Drawings Room & The Hyman Kreitman Reading Rooms at Tate Britain, the Tate Stores, Andrew Teverson, David Thompson, The Times Literary Supplement, Alice Tyrell, Warren Von Eschenbach, Anya Wojnowicz, the students & staff at The University of Notre Dame, the residents & staff at Edward Alleyn House, Cafe Viva in Peckham & Robert Young Antiques.

For permissions to reproduce the paintings I would like to thank the Tate Gallery, the Wallace Collection and the Yale Center for British Art, Paul Mellon Collection.

For permission to reproduce the frontispiece of the 1949 catalogue of Dr. H.A.C. Gregory's paintings at auction I would like to thank Sotheby's Picture Gallery and for permission to reproduce materials relating to Dr. H.A.C. Gregory and his involvement with the first Aldeburgh Festival I would like to thank the Britten-Pears Library.
For permission to include the poems, 'Dream', 'The Gardener' & 'The Return of the Herd' I would like to thank Poetry Review, The Rialto & Rufus Books.

I would like to thank Alice Solomons at Free Association Books for believing in my book and for her professionalism and encouragement throughout the publishing process.
Especial thanks to my mother, Dinah Gregory (1927 – 2014), my sister, Liz, my brother, Robert, and Lucy, Oscar & Pablo for their love, companionship and belief in my work.

Illustrations

Preface

Children frequently manifest a desire to exhibit. [1]

(Sigmund Freud)

n *The Interpretation of Dreams* (1900) Freud writes that in dreams the adult may recover the 'Paradise' of a child's uninhibited nature and the immense joy he once experienced in the exhibition of his nakedness. 'One can scarcely pass through a country village in our part of the world,' Freud recalls, 'without meeting some child of two or three who lifts up his little shirt in front of one'. Over a hundred years later, in the place of Freud's boy, I see a girl who is much more tentative about such an exhibition. She prefers to stay inside and play with her toys.

I continue reading from Book IV (*The Interpretation of Dreams I*) of the Standard Edition of Freud's works. I inherited these volumes from my late father, Dr. Basil Gregory (1920 – 1990), whose papers (finished and unfinished), Joanne Halford (the archivist at the Institute

---

[1] Sigmund Freud, 'Typical Dreams', 244, IV (1900), *The Standard Edition of the Complete Psychological Works of Sigmund Freud*, translated from the German under the General Editorship of James Strachey, The Hogarth Press & The Institute of Psycho-analysis, London (1953)

of Psychoanalysis in Maida Vale) has recently catalogued as a memorial holding in recognition of my father's work in psychiatry and as the first Director pioneering group psychoanalytic therapy at the Paddington Day Hospital (NHS) in the 1960s.[2]

I am browsing through my father's volumes almost a quarter of a century after his death, gleaning ideas that I greet as old familiars: as a child of psychoanalysis I recognise the ideas I inherited mostly unconsciously at my father's knee. I have not read Freud extensively and in this book about pictures I dip into the volumes like a child getting newly acquainted with some old books that were part of the furniture in her family home.

> When we look back at this unashamed period of childhood it seems to us a Paradise; and Paradise itself is no more than a group phantasy of the childhood of the individual. That is why mankind were naked in Paradise and were without shame in one another's presence; till a moment arrived when shame and anxiety awoke, expulsion followed, and sexual life and the tasks of cultural activity began. But we can regain this Paradise every night in our dreams. I have already [p. 218] expressed a suspicion that impressions of earliest childhood (that is, from the prehistoric epoch until about the end of the third year of life) strive to achieve reproduction, from their very nature and irrespectively perhaps of their actual content, and that their repetition constitutes the fulfilment of a wish. Thus dreams of being naked are dreams of exhibiting. [3]

We can regain this Paradise every night in our dreams. My dreams (those I remember) have often been disturbed and fearful, and I am growing more aware of the deep sense of guardedness that has been apparent in much of my waking life, but also in the realm of my dreams. Even as a patient in psychoanalytic psychotherapy over a very productive twelve year period, that guardedness has maintained a strong hold on my mind.

---

[2] P42, Institute of Psychoanalysis archive

[3] Freud, 245, IV, ibid

I have rarely stumbled into Freud's paradise when in deep sleep, but if I have done so without recalling the dream, I am glad.

In a review of my collection of poems, *In Slow Woods*, the poet and critic, Valeria Melchioretto, writes of the voice in my poetry 'melting down time and space to fashion a fluid wakefulness as it usually only occurs in dreams.'[4] Her words are helpful. This is the closest I am aware of getting to the 'prehistoric epoch', the 'paradise' of a small child's imagination. The paintings I discuss in this book are like dreams that play upon my waking mind. I have enjoyed their presence in precious solitude over many years. My mind has, though, in recent times grown rather over- full of pictures so I have gathered them here inside the covers of this book, as though to secure the legacy, the pictures in my mind that I may pass on down the line. Each chapter is like a separate room in the many suites of paintings I stroll through in my imagination, laying my thoughts and feelings bare in their presence.

Freud's Standard Edition is in twenty-four volumes and, as I show you my pictures, these books are in every room of my gallery. Some lie open on the floor and others are on an unobtrusive shelf. This book, *The Studio*, is divided into eleven chapters and an Afterword. There are twenty-four hours in one day and one night. I write my book by day and begin to let go of the script at bedtime. In dreams I begin not to write. I begin to be a child again.

I stand before my readers like a child in their eyes. Here is a story of paintings and of myself that needs to be given an airing. There are pictures in my mind – the evidence of a great deal of covert 'cultural activity', adult musings and thoughts that draw upon the 'paradise' the child in me (naked as the day) has dreamt and now brings to light. They are sensual and erotic and convey the scents of a garden in my thoughts. I would like very much to share these with you. First, though, I need to recall a little of my past and recent present as a preamble to entering into the exhibition.

---

[4] Valeria Melchioretto, 'To sleep, perchance to dream – ay, there's the poetry', 141 – 143, *Tears in the Fence* (54), 2012

I grew up in a small Surrey village with an elder sibling (by two years) who suffered from a very severe form of epilepsy. I have written in another book[5] (from a child's point of view) about growing up with my brother, Andrew, but only now (as an adult narrator) do I recognise that the experience of my early childhood has lodged in my mind and soul, perpetuating in adulthood the feeling of being forever arrested and interrupted at the root of my being. I have been stopped in my child-tracks in the face of my brother's unremitting seizures. It was as if time stood still in his presence and, as a result, my child-mind and my adult-mind were severely curtailed in the freedoms so necessary to growth. With the help of a very patient and insightful analytic therapist, I grappled with those seizures, the seemingly never-ending series of petit mal that had taken hold in my mind. I have shared my dear brother's seizures day in and day out – when he was alive and in my life after his death at the age of twenty-six in 1977. Carefree pleasures were forever being halted in our play and over the years I began to forget what it had ever felt like to let myself go. I have waited and watched for the seizures to pass.

Even though, with the help of my therapist, I eventually developed an academic career and established myself as a writer, part of me is still engaged with bringing that early child self into freer and fuller expression. For the past twenty years or so I have explored and played with paintings and their impressions, but I have shared this keenest of joys with only a few. I have been extremely tentative about revealing my pleasure. I have wandered, in secret, around art galleries as though they were Freud's idea of Paradise, the dream of an unguarded early life mingling with the actual childhood memories stirred by the pictures I have found. I have hidden the secret of my pleasure.

Virginia Woolf writes that 'on first entering a picture gallery' she experienced the 'stillness, warmth and seclusion from the perils of the street'. She finds herself in a 'primeval forest'.[6] My 'gallery' is similarly

---

[5] Gill Gregory, *The Sound of Turquoise*, KUP, 2009/2010

[6] Virginia Woolf, *Walter Sickert: a conversation* (1934), Tate Publishing, 2005

warm and secluded, but not so much 'primeval' as like a gentle wooded English park, a relatively 'tame' place where pictures are placed upon the branches of trees.

I have been too 'wakeful' and on the alert for much of my life, but at the age of just turned sixty-one I seem to be finding my way more freely in the world. For twelve years I was a patient in psychoanalytic therapy and this long period of very fruitful therapy came to a conclusion in 1999. During those twelve years I attained a PhD in Victorian poetry and wrote a critical biography.[7]. In the course of the next twelve years I wrote many poems along with *The Sound of Turquoise* and *In Slow Woods*. I developed my lecturing at The University of Notre Dame in London where my many students have, over the sixteen years I have taught there, stood in the place of the children I might have cherished. In the past couple of years I have picked up where I left off in my therapy, this time with a male therapist, Mario Guarnieri. He is very interested in 'play' and this current semester I am beginning to skip in my dreams.

Only last week I found myself on Rye Lane in Peckham, near where my therapist practises, watching the world go by. That expression has never made much sense to me. I have not watched the world go by in my life from the vantage point of a street cafe in Paris or a coffee house in Peckham or from anywhere I have happened to be. I have been much too conflicted, preoccupied and acutely anxious to relax my mind. I seem to have arrived at a place where I am gathering strength daily and am really looking about me. In the final chapter of this book, 'A Studio in Paris', I discuss a painting by the Futurist, C.R.W. Nevinson, of a young naked woman looking out from her studio at the rooftops of Paris. She is unashamed. She is my dream of 'exhibiting' and of awakening desire. This young woman is myself and in writing this book I have arrived at her Parisian point of view. I have a keen sense of her waking body and soul.

---

[7] Gill Gregory, *The Life & Work of Adelaide Procter: poetry, feminism & fathers*, Ashgate, 1998

These paintings have returned me to the 'paradise', the 'prehistoric' imagination Freud imagines, but I am a girl who has only very recently learned to be more confident. I find a child's long stalled expression in the light of these pictures. I begin to know myself again and again and again in attending to the details of their composition. I do sometimes possess the cheekiness of Freud's small boy and this childlike naughtiness combines with a deep and more adult awareness of the pleasures I am learning to enjoy more fully without too many interruptions.

Writing this book has coincided with a move I made last November from a home of twenty years on the Clapham-Brixton borders to a studio at the heart of a beautiful village, a pastoral enclave in south east London. Here in this wonderfully light room I have gathered together these paintings I love.

In the wise words of John Berger, 'Here is where we meet' [8] every day.

I hope my spectators, my readers, will tread lightly. These are (after all) my dreams and 'their repetition constitutes the fulfilment of a wish'. [9] Fulfilment (for myself) has not come easily but I am now waking on many a morning with a delightful sense of anticipation as to where my pictures will take me next. I have stepped into each day as though it were new unto itself. I have lived in an ever-changing present and have found myself at liberty to lay my soul bare.

I have moved to a place that reminds me of the 'country village' of my childhood. Here are masses of trees of all shapes and sizes. Walking to and from the station (where I take a train to London Bridge on my way to work near Trafalgar Square) is a pleasure that keeps being repeated. Late at night, having been out for the evening, I walk back to my studio from the last train that pulls into the small station. The train arrives a minute before midnight and I and a few other travellers wend our ways home. Repetition is reassuring. Repetition is wonderful. Repetition is necessary to survival. This I continue to learn in my burgeoning experience of psychoanalytic engagement,

---

[8] John Berger, *Here Is Where We Meet: A Story of Crossing Paths*, Vintage, 2006

[9] Freud, 245, IV, ibid

in the course of which arriving and leaving, entering and exiting the therapist's room, become profound acts of commitment to the ordinary processes involved in getting well.

My therapists (past and present) and I (their patient) take care of the small child in our midst. She is a picture of lack in her early life: for liberty she gasps. This village and the train are like the toys I never truly played with in the presence of my brother's painful and preoccupying epilepsy. He has been at rest since 1977, but my memory of him has filled my mind and heart and soul for what seems like an eternity and now I must let go of Andrew. I have loved him so much (hated him too and that is such a very hard feeling) whilst standing in the shadow of those seizures. I love him today as a diffused presence in among the trees where I live. The reverberations of his seizures are absorbed by and begin to disappear in the greenery all around me.

The tree-lined street through the village is gently lit and on my way home from that late night train, I stroll past the small shops in an enveloping darkness, as if I were held in a lover's arms – the arms perhaps of a beautiful young man I met last year at a conference on lyric at the University of London. He is a poet and natural philosopher from New York and his name is Zohar, the Hebrew word for 'radiance'. He is around thirty and I am sixty-one. I am twice his age but we meet in my early childhood, loving a world full of pictures and poems and their ideas. His beauty and robust health are striking. He is my idea of a more lyrical future.

I pick up my pen inside a studio in a row of almshouses. Writing has filled my life and I am beginning to realise that the printed word and the pictures I write about (Freud's 'cultural activity') are (at the end of the day) simply art and beautifully removed (a few steps away) from life itself and relationship. My studio in Dulwich is an artful reality: my rooms are on the upper storey (there are just two storeys which keeps things simple) and close by there is a chapel (built in the seventeenth century) which opens into the cloisters on one side and on the other into Dulwich Picture Gallery, a small and perfectly formed house of art. One room leads to another and parts of myself connect and re-connect in this place of settlement and history and art. I begin to move away from the shadows of my brother's epilepsy. I am gathering myself.

Here in this little enclave I can (for as long as it takes, perhaps, to write this book) feel secure and integral to the fabric of the building, the settlement that holds me in place.

In a studio I sit at my newly installed Swedish work station and here I become a time traveller steering a course through paintings, with Freud's twenty-four volumes at my fingertips, a treasury of ideas and inspirations, but not my Bible. My time machine is compact but strong enough to carry such weighty tomes, and some of the books are scattered on its floor. I am on the verge of entering more wholeheartedly into my world of paintings which become stepping stones in a search to locate myself in the outside world.

I look out from my three tall and elegant windows (two in the studio room and one in the kitchen) onto a large gate that opens into a late nineteenth-century park, which was in turn opened by the Whig politician, Lord Rosebery. The park is beautifully maintained and has a lake at its heart. East of the lake there is an American garden well-known for its mass of rhododendrons that blossom in May. The Queen Mary Gate close by commemorates the visits Mary of Teck (George V's consort) paid every spring to see the flowers blossoming. In taking Freud's 'royal road to the unconscious' I have arrived at a place that is a picture. In a sense this village is a picture postcard and I wish my friends and my therapists, my students and my family were here. The rooms are comfortable and the sky and its changing colours are ever-present.

People and many dogs walk and run in this green space, revelling in its relative freedom from the high octane urban tensions in close proximity. Foxes come and go after the park closes for the night. Many live in Dulwich Woods, their natural habitat, and the ones I've seen (often in the corner of my eye as they dart across the road) look sleek and healthy, their red coats shining in the darkness. Their wildness can be borne in mind without threatening to tear me apart, whisk me away, as of old. That story of abandonment and addiction has been immensely tiring. It is old as the hills where I leave it to rest.

The first New Year I spent here ten months ago we were inches deep in snow and this village was like a fairytale alighting in the midst of urban densities. The red, single-decker bus – the only bus to pass through the village – is appropriately small and toy-like: it kept going even with all the snow, the tyres warming and melting the ice. In the presence of the small bus I am reminded of my mother reading me *The Little Train That Could*. I think I can. I think I can. I think I can. The little train puffs up a steep hill, willing itself toward the summit and the relief of the down slope.[10]

I collect pictures as if they were the cards in a child's sweet wrapper. I am in the tradition of collectors on each side of my family, who appear inside the covers of my book. We are like siblings who are at liberty to share an early passion. I have (to my astonishment) discovered Frank Stoop (deceased) and his bequest[11] in the Tate archive in the past year - a kindred spirit (childless like myself) on my mother's side of the family. On my father's side there is a little Russian grandfather (he was very short)[12] who carelessly, in his rapturous desire for pictures, 'lost' a painting by John Constable that was thankfully 'found' by the Tate Gallery. We three collectors enjoy the pictures playing in our minds. We are in 'Paradise' again.

Each chapter holds a picture to the light and, as I look into each painting, a child's small world opens up in my view. Come, take my hand – let me show you around.

---

[10] Rev. Charles S. Wing, 'Story of the Engine that Thought it Could', *New York Tribune*, 8.4.1906

[11] *The Stoop Bequest*, 1933, Tate Gallery Archive

[12] My book, *The Sound of Turquoise*, imagines my grandfather's escape from Tashkent circa 1904

1

The Arab Tent

Children have no scruples over allowing animals to rank as their full equals. Uninhibited as they are in the avowal of their bodily needs, they no doubt feel themselves more akin to animals than to their elders, who may well be a puzzle to them.[13]

The tagine was aromatic, lovely. The taste and texture of the olives and meat, the tomatoes and light couscous, linger on my tongue. It was cold and wet outside but warm inside the restaurant in the village a minute's walk from my studio. There was a scattering of people in the large room and I felt comfortable eating my meal at four in the afternoon.

Four o'clock was tea-time in my childhood, when our family of six, along with the six cats, gathered by a log fire in winter, eating toast and honey, chocolate cake and flapjacks, accompanied by freshly brewed, strong Indian tea. Our mother, purveyor and overseer, watched over this gathering whilst our father, the psychoanalytic psychiatrist, ate slowly as though he were forever contemplating the food he enjoyed. His twenty-four volumes of Freud were displayed on the bookcase in

---

[13] Sigmund Freud, 'Return of Totemism in Childhood', 127, XIII (1913 – 1914) ibid

an alcove beside the hearth. I always found the sight of their dark blue covers comforting and intriguing and magical. The books invoked my father's presence in his absence. His work as a full-time consultant at Horton (a large psychiatric hospital in Epsom) and as an analyst in training in London, kept my father away from home for much of the time. Even when he was at home he seemed eternally preoccupied. From when I was a small child, I was very aware of my father's distant look, as though he was always elsewhere in his thoughts. Freud's books, though, along with works by Franz Kafka and Rebecca West, were there on the shelves and now they are on mine.

Most of all, though, I was aware of my brother, Andrew, fearing that a seizure may this time end with him falling into the fire, which (in an increasingly tortured adolescence) he often stoked to a dangerously roaring blaze, or with him crashing down onto the trolley laden with food. This never did happen, but tea-time was regularly, monotonously interrupted by the petit mal that came thick and fast. Andrew would stand or sit stock-still, his poor body rigid and jerking in what seemed an interminable series of seizures. He rarely lost his balance and, when he returned to 'normal', we all resumed eating, intent on drawing no attention to the hard, staccato interruptions. We shared Andrew's terrible pain and suffering, and returned to our food as though his life depended on us wiping our plates clean.

In retrospect I realise just how petrified I was in Andrew's presence (as were my much smaller brother and sister in their turn). I see myself turning to stone where I sat. My belief (bordering on superstition) in Freud's tomes, my father's books, could not prevent such petrifaction.

The cats (three generations) either eyed Andrew and the seizures from the comfort of an armchair or ran beneath the grand piano, cowering until the all clear was sounded by the returning clink of cutlery and the murmur of deliberately light conversation. The cats moved among us, tabby, black and tortoise-shell, watching out for scraps or jumping up onto someone's knee. I welcomed their warmth and liveliness as I had delighted in the kittens they once were. When on my own with them I could even feel relatively 'uninhibited' and felt a freedom in allowing them to climb all over me. At eight years old I played with a litter of kittens on my silky eiderdown, loving their young animal breath and the little teeth that nibbled my fingers –the nuzzle of their small noses and the erotic, sensual purring.

After the tagine in Dulwich I sipped jasmine tea, resting my head against imaginary cushions, Berber style. Something was nuzzling my foot. I looked down to see a golden retriever (a puppy) snuffling for food. I had nothing to offer and, after I had patted her head and tickled her ears, she returned to her owner, an elderly man in a corner. An animated couple were in another corner and every so often they looked over at me and smiled. They were African, Eritrean possibly from the look of their delicate, finely chiselled features, and seemed incongruous in this predominantly 'white' village. They appeared to be very at home in their corner as did the old man and his retriever. I was by the wall down the middle of the room and equidistant from both sets of diners.

There were Marc Chagall exhibition posters on the walls – animals and dancing figures, upside down people and flowers. My first therapist had Chagall on her walls and here they were again in my view.

Today this eating house felt like a tent full of sleepy life – rather like the house of a Berber boy in Marrakesh I once knew. Aged nineteen, I was touring Northern Africa with a friend, Carol, and we met two boys who took us on their scooters to the desert and back again to a warm house furnished with cushions and carpets and throws. We kissed a little and slept after taking our meal, cross-legged, on a rug. There was a black cat somewhere in the room. She mewed every so often but stayed on her own. Those lyrical boys in my past took root in my mind and in my body's memory, even though I cast them out of my mind after Andrew died in 1977. That was my sacrifice. No-one could or would replace my brother. The Berber boys (my heart purring) were set aside.

I could have stayed in the Dulwich Village restaurant (that tent full of animals) much longer but left after an hour. I felt so relaxed I might have slept a little in its quiet hold.

I returned to my studio to continue thinking about pictures and animals. I have a large print of Edwin Landseer's *The Arab Tent* on a wall in my small, bright kitchen, the tall window filling the room with light and framing the large trees outside. Everywhere I walk in this studio there are trees. *The Arab Tent* is beside the fridge and faces me, warms me, when I come out of the kitchen into the sitting and sleeping area. I have lived with this picture for twenty years now and I love it perhaps more than I can say. I have not had it framed yet as if I and the picture were 'nomadic' and still waiting to settle. *The Arab Tent* is a picture of animals and I feel akin to them. They nourish my soul, take the chill out of my spirit.

The painting is dated 1866 (when Freud was a ten year old child – did that boy dream of animals? I wonder), the year the work was first exhibited at the Royal Academy as *Mare and Foal – Indian Tent.* Landseer was the foremost Victorian painter of animals, much loved by the public and by Queen Victoria.

There is still some uncertainty as to the tent's origins. When it was first shown at the Royal Academy, *The Times* pointed out that Landseer had chosen to call it an Indian tent but 'it should rather be called an Arab tent, having regard to its material, colour and occupants.'[14] It is not surprising Landseer got the title wrong, given he rarely painted the oriental subjects that were fashionable at the time. Landseer is more usually associated with English and Scottish animals – hounds and horses and stags, his 'monarchs of the glen'. His most well-known works today, though, are the bronze lions that took up residence at the base of Nelson's column in Trafalgar Square in 1867, just six years before Landseer died in 1873 (having been declared 'insane' in the summer of 1872).

I pass Landseer's lions every morning, tuning in to their benign peacefulness at the base of Nelson's column (a kind of totem pole) on my way to lecture at The University of Notre Dame, the college building being near the National Gallery's Sainsbury Wing. They look

[14] John Ingamells, *The Wallace Collection Catalogue of Pictures*, I, 1985

so benign I forget the real lion pacing and stalking, sleeping and mating, in far off climes. The bronze and the stone of the square, along with its military heroes, mute their animal power and, even though I love the lions and the gentleness Landseer moulded, ideas of the wild and its concomitant freedoms and fears remain elsewhere.

The animals in *The Arab Tent* are also un-wild but they possess the warmth and liveliness a painting (unlike sculpture) is able to convey. This picture is the next best thing to animals in the flesh. I see them in the 'Paradise' imagined by Freud. In 2002 the picture was highlighted by the Wallace Collection as *Treasure of the Month*.

Landseer and his childhood friend, John Frederick Lewis, [15] at the age of twelve would walk to the Exeter Exchange on the Strand to visit the menagerie of exotic animals, who were often resting after a gruelling circus tour. Side by side the friends copied the animals and then later Lewis went further afield, finding a comfortable 'oriental' billet in Cairo for ten years where he painted unseen and well away from the London art market. He escaped the overwhelming burden of popularity, which exacerbated Landseer's fragile psyche to the point of insanity and a sad death.

When I first saw *The Arab Tent* (completed in 1866, a year before Landseer's lions appeared) in the early 1990s, I was at the beginning of my journey into art and psychoanalysis. I sensed that paintings were becoming important to me and my processes, but I would have been surprised to learn that twenty years later I would be living in a village next door to a gallery, and that paintings would have moved to the centre of my writing life.

I came upon *The Arab Tent* in the spring of 1992 when I was attending a day school at the Institute of Psychoanalysis, where my father had trained as an analyst for ten years in the sixties. Paula Heimann was his analyst, whom he both feared and loved so far I could sense. He barely talked of his analysis. On the cusp of death, he would laugh ruefully and affectionately, 'There was a picture of a strutting cock

---

[15] A painting by John Frederick Lewis is explored in Ch 2

on her waiting-room wall!'

I was visiting the Institute for the first time and was excited at entering my father's spiritual home where I would meet members of his psychoanalytic clan. He had died two years earlier in 1990, relieved to know that at last I had embarked on a psychoanalytic journey of my own. His own remained unfinished as in the early 1970s he left the analysis, resigned as Director of Paddington Day Hospital (the NHS experiment in group psychoanalytic therapy, my father appointed its first Director in 1962) and returned to work full-time as a consultant at Horton Hospital in Epsom. He had not turned against psychoanalysis, but life (most tellingly in the form of Andrew's illness, which was growing much worse) had got the better of him. He remained loyal and deeply attached to the psychoanalytic endeavour until his death and passed that love and strong attachment on to me, his eldest daughter.

At the time of the day school the Institute was in New Cavendish Street south of Regent's Park. The school was on literature and its psychoanalytic qualities, focussing in particular on George Eliot's *Middlemarch*, 1874, a large and generous novel full of people and animals and rich farmland. I'd fallen in love with Eliot's fertile imagination when studying English A Level at school in the late sixties. In the lunch break I visited the Wallace Collection in Manchester Square, a Georgian garden square a few minutes' walk away from the Institute.

I did not get any further than the entrance hall to Hertford House, the home of the Wallace Collection, which was bequeathed to the nation by Julie Amelie Charlotte Castelnau, the widow of Richard Wallace, in 1890 on the condition that the whole collection remain in the building, as though this was a very special and sequestered gathering. My attention was arrested by Landseer's *The Arab Tent* (c. 1865 – 1866) which hangs in the hall. I was surprised by its exquisitely lyrical beauty and studied the painting for a good ten minutes before the doorman noticed my interest and arrived at my side.

He began telling me about the picture, recounting the story of its provenance with great good humour. I sensed his affection and admiration for the work was longstanding. He might have been the animals' devoted keeper. I wonder if he still works there – probably not as he must have been well into his sixties then, which would make him well into his eighties now. If he is alive, I wish him happiness in his retirement. I hope he is comfortable wherever he is. I have liked and looked up to many doormen in my life, most recently another tall man, Louis Nelson, who guards the door of my college. He is in training as a counsellor and is modest about his ambitions. Louis begins and ends my day and sometimes he returns from visiting relations in Jamaica, bearing a book of poems, a gift for me from his homeland. Before quoting the doorman at the Wallace, I shall describe what I see today in *The Arab Tent* when I look at it in my kitchen, taking the animals in semi-consciously as I move to and fro between meals.

The large picture is in oils and it depicts a cream coloured mare sitting in the foreground of the tent, with a brown foal curved into her body. The mare's mouth rests on her foal's rump as though she were kissing it gently. The picture is one of contentment. The animals are seated on an eastern carpet (a kind of magic carpet) which is a muted red colour with a blue and off-white symmetrical pattern. The tent is coloured brown and gold and on its roof there are palm fronds and two monkeys, one asleep and clutching an orange whilst the other, a black monkey, is awake and on the alert. To the left of the mare and foal there is a fire burning in a brass brazier and just behind them to the right there are two greyhounds resting on a blue-grey, red-striped rug and a cheetah skin. To their right you can see two oriental pipes in a green jar.

I often wonder if the animals are alone in this warm, sleepy scene. Is their owner a few feet away outside the frame looking in on his animals? Why has Landseer drawn this combination of animals in one small tent? Perhaps the tent is not small and this scene is in the corner of a much larger tent. Maybe the tent belongs to a travelling circus or caravan of animals en route to a market where they will be sold, each perhaps going to a different owner and the company of animals broken up. They all look well watered and nourished.

The tent reminds me of Freud's consulting room in Vienna and I am in turn reminded of the warmth and feeling of kinship I often experience inside the therapy tent. At regular intervals I talk with my therapist about cats and the occasional dog. I tell him about this picture and he listens quietly to the details. Psychoanalysis is most potent as a listening therapy, not a 'talking cure' with the therapist well armed with 'interpretations'. He listens and I find my way into the words I speak, or I listen to him listening to me and, in the process, come closest to the words (spoken or unspoken) that ring most true. I listen to myself in his presence. Sometimes there is light conversation which feels rather like taking a pleasant meal. Fighting and anger were very much at the heart of my past therapy but I am beginning to say goodbye to all that noise.

I look forward to my next meal in my Italian therapist's tent. He came highly recommended and (to my astonishment) I learned that his consulting room was in Holly Grove, Peckham, the same street where I lived for a few months in 1971, at the age of nineteen, in a Maoist 'cell'. I cannot remember which house I and my 'comrades' lived in but, on that first visit to my therapist, Mario Guarnieri, I was struck by the memories of Peckham flooding back, particularly the scents of the many cosmopolitan foods on offer in Rye Lane and its markets. One strong memory is of a fellow Maoist and I being arrested for sticking up posters for a May Day parade. The police had skidded to a halt around midnight and caught us in the act under the bridge at Peckham Rye station. We were charged and I was fined £5 (so far as I remember) and advised by the Bow Street magistrate to 'keep on the right side of the law or you'll end up in Holloway, young lady!'

When I first met my therapist on the doorstep of his rooms in his basement cave I wondered if this was the very same house I had once lived in. He looked Asian, even though his name is Italian and, when he began to speak in his comfortable consulting room, I noticed his Northern English accent. Later I would discover that he is from Manchester (via Italy). His garden (paved in places and full of flowers and plants) and the large, long haired cat that often basked in the sun on the floor of his waiting-room reminded me of courtyards in Marrakesh and of the Berber boys. I lay on my Italian's couch and partook of his food.

> *Customs still in force among the Arabs of the desert show that what is binding in a common meal is not a religious factor but the act of eating itself. Anyone who has eaten the smallest morsel of food with one of these Bedouin or has swallowed a mouthful of his milk need no longer fear him as an enemy but may feel secure in his protection and help. Not, however, for an unlimited time; strictly speaking, only so long as the food which has been eaten in common remains in the body. Such was the realistic view of the bond of union. It needed repetition in order to be confirmed and made permanent.*[16]

The arrangement of Landseer's *The Arab Tent* was probably imagined in the London painter's studio – a studio not unlike my own studio or the Peckham therapy tent in which I share my ideas and emotions in a 'bond of union' for the duration of the fifty minutes. Freud's 'Return of Totemism in Childhood' explores the centrality of animals to early totemic cultures. He distinguishes 'a fetish' from 'a totem' in that the totem 'is never an isolated individual, but always a class of objects, generally a species of animals'.[17] The members of a clan are bound together by their 'totem' which is passed from one generation to the next. Some clans have 'pictures of animals painted or tattooed on their bodies'.[18]

There are animals wandering in and out of my thoughts. I am a member of a clan.

The Arab Tent on my kitchen wall is like an early totem. Each picture discussed in this book and with my therapist is one of a circle of 'objects' that form part of a totem. I can carry these pictures around, bear them

---

[16] Sigmund Freud, 'Return of Totemism in Childhood', 134, XIII ibid

[17] 103, XIII ibid

[18] 101, XIII ibid

in mind. They nourish and refresh my imagination for as long as the idea remains in my body – the idea of a secular and sensual communion. My therapist presides over the meal and its need of repetition. At other times I preside. I am older than my therapist and have travelled the world. I am his elder and a woman of the world. He sits at the end of the couch and listens to me. I and my young man chew things over.

However sparse or occasionally stodgy the meal might be, it is important that we partake. Its idea is central to the therapy. Sometimes we celebrate a feast but that is rare. In the moment of sharing it does not matter where he or I are from in respect of our histories or geographies. Some days I arrive without memory or desire, only to find them both in the course of the therapy hour, the fifty minutes of psychoanalytic therapy, which allows time (ten full minutes) to arrive and take my leave. Sometimes I make a graceful departure, bidding my Italian farewell, meeting his eyes. At others I am too full of emotion and words yet to be expressed to hold my poise and then I leave quickly like a frightened child. On those occasions I often cannot wait to get back to my writing and research. I return to the written word and its immense consolations.

The art historian, Dr. Peter A. Andrews, writes in a letter (22nd October 2001) to Stephen Duffy, (the curator of nineteenth-century paintings at the Wallace at that time) that even though the tent does appear to be more Arabic than Indian, it is not possible to be conclusive.[19] Maybe there is no need of being 'conclusive'. Names and titles can often put a lid on freer expression. Landseer went mad when he became too well-known. *The Arab Tent* is a gathering of animals in privacy. They are not, in that moment, bothered about their origins. I love this gathering and long to share my pleasure with a like-minded friend.

'The picture glows, doesn't it?!' the doorman had winked at me.

Yes and it still glows in my kitchen, I answer him today. Back then, over twenty years ago, I did not trust my own responses to art. I could not believe in our shared communion.

He began.

---

[19] Letter from Dr. Peter A. Andrews to Mr. Stephen Duffy, 10.11.01

'Do you know who bought the painting?'

No, I didn't.

'None other than the Prince of Wales, known as Bertie, later Edward VII. He bought the picture in 1867 for 1,500 guineas and then Sir Richard Wallace purchased it in 1878 for £7,912! Sir Richard was desperate to have the picture and it was the most expensive work of art bought by the founders of the collection.'

He smiled down at me. He was about six feet tall and his greying hair was short, cropped. His square face was tanned, as if he had been enjoying the desert sun along with the animals. He looked well travelled and had an alert, brisk demeanour. Maybe he was ex-services and had arrived at a well earned billet beside the door of this secluded building facing its square of mature, sunlit trees. Perhaps he was finally taking some rest after a lifetime of toil. What a joy to feast on *The Arab Tent* day after day and for the art-food to miraculously appear each time he grew hungry for another look.

The doorman continued.

'Once Sir Richard had passed and his widow gifted the entire collection to the nation, the doors opened to the public in 1900. No object in this house must ever leave the collection, even for loan exhibitions.'

Were the pictures prisoners? I wondered. Or did they feel rather special in this small, secluded spot? Here they were inside their museum-cave, a treasure.

He looked wistful. Maybe, like me, he'd like to tuck *The Arab Tent* under his arm and steal her away in the night. A picture such as this might be happily ensconced in the most modest of lodgings or studios, even if it took up most of one wall. We could steal away with the picture in the night after closing time without anyone noticing. Surely the Wallace trusted their doorman to lock up after him. Our ownership of this fine piece would seem entirely natural hanging modestly in our kitchen. And then he smiled and laughed.

'Sir Richard had the Great Gallery built on top of the stables downstairs!'

I was standing in the stables. I wondered what his name was. George or Anthony. I decided on George like our new-born prince. His nice brown eyes shone. We stood side by side admiring the painting and after a minute or so he walked back to his post by the stable door.

But I had to get back to the Institute, Sigmund Freud on their walls (I was very much in awe of my father's head tribesman back then) for another talk on the Victorian writer, George Eliot (aka Marian Evans). Another George. The doorman at the Wallace reminded me of my idea of Eliot, who possesses such a humane and intelligent voice in her fiction. Tone is important, whether it belongs to a doorman or a therapist, an analyst or a writer. Like a gathering of animals we meet as kindred spirits in our mutual tones.

The painting would not disappear unless there was a fire and the building burnt to cinders. I was reminded of my elder brother, Andrew, standing over the fire stoking it to a bonfire blaze that might have burnt the house down. I imagined the fire brigade arriving (like the shiny red Dinky toy Andrew guarded closely) and rescuing visitors trapped inside. The doorman would be at the helm of the rescue and would surely save *The Arab Tent* for posterity. Animals and children first. I am glad the picture is placed in the entrance hall, as if it were on the way out of a mother's precious womb and into the world outside. *The Arab Tent* is wary of its well established neighbours – the Old Masters and the shining armour, the Limoges enamels, the silver snuffboxes and bronze nymphs. The animals find such company rather stuffy and lacking in vitality. They prefer a sunset glow in the desert to the sparkle of jewels in a safe.

The speaker at the Institute of Psychoanalysis talked about the maturity of George Eliot's compassionate and analytic imagination – an imagination that accommodated necessary failures along with the unnecessary, the reality of a lack of fulfilment (in varying degrees) that may be found in most lives. Her plotting of English provincial life (a place of farms and their animals in many of her novels) is extraordinary and the lecturer (a psychoanalyst) urged us to read and re-read Eliot to appreciate the love that lay at the core of her vision.

Only repeated readings would secure her compassion's strong hold on the heart and mind.

When I returned to my flat in Clapham that evening it was *The Arab Tent* that lingered uppermost in my mind. I grew jealous of my picture. The doorman was very lucky to see her every day. Were the mare and her foal waiting for me and my doorman (the animals' caretakers) to return and share those two pipes in the green jar?

Suddenly in my musings I see my family of six in the picture. The orange in the sleeping monkey's hand is a sphere of belonging. The fruit is sacred, part of a totem that ensures the clan's safety in perpetuity. My mother is the beautiful mare presiding and the foal is Andrew, her first born who died at the young age of twenty-six. The foal in the painting looks delicate but not racked by seizures and insurmountable rage, whose appetite was gargantuan. He has quietened and found calm in his mother's care. The sleeping greyhounds are my much loved younger siblings, the brother and sister who ran like the wind beneath blue skies, one beside the other. I envied their freedom and ordinary companionship as I sat in the shadows of my brother's terrible illness. In the tent we come together, a clan in my eyes. We are bound by the objects, the totem in our view. We shall protect each other and partake of familial love.

The monkeys are in a fold of the tent above the sibling dogs. The monkeys are my father and myself, united in our love of psychoanalytic ideas and their fruit. My father holds onto the orange, the totem, in his sleep. He died over twenty years ago after several strokes but he is restored in the picture on my kitchen wall. I am the other monkey in jet-black, the colour of my half Russian father's hair when he was young. The black monkey is vigilant, keeping a watch in case our tent is not safe. She is the gatekeeper but there is no gate, only an aperture in the cloth. The animals are relatively free to come and go as they please. There will be no animal sacrifice in this twenty-first century clan. I am almost a vegetarian these days, only eating fish and barely any meat.

The black monkey must, though, still keep her watch. Our family name, Gregory, has a root meaning in Greek of 'watchful'. The word possesses the power of a totem: 'to watch' is our byword. The black monkey is mindful that her tired father is sleeping, perhaps on the cusp of death. She is aware that the foal in his mother's arms will die young. She is already in mourning. This memory tent and its relaxed but alert atmosphere are surely not in danger, though. The two pipes are waiting for their owners to return and then they'll have a smoke by the hearth. The owners might be any couple who notice *The Arab Tent* as they pass through the hallway at the Wallace Collection, and then stop to look at the picture long enough to take in its fertile tones and suggestions. Maybe the monkey can relax her hold after all.

I anticipate sharing the picture and its associations at my therapist's table. I will talk with him of this gathering of animals on my kitchen wall, taking them in as I prepare rice and pine-nuts, vegetables and fruit, for my evening meal. This clan of animals is not (as Freud asserts) a substitute for the father ('Psycho-analysis has revealed that the totem animal is in reality a substitute for the father').[20] The father (a century after Freud) is less patriarchal. He is among us, holding onto the orange, the family totem. None of us, at this moment of my contemplating the picture, will apportion and eat the segments. We are well nourished and content. All in good time, eventually, we will share the totem, the token, and give thanks. I and my version of this family will step out of the picture and into the wider world.

In the next picture you can hear a low murmuring of people and the sounds of ever-present animals and birds. The picture encompasses a wider view.

SOURCES

John Ingamells, *The Wallace Collection, Catalogue of Pictures*, I, 1985

Treasure of the Month: Edwin Landseer, The Arab Tent, The Wallace Collection, January 2002

S. Duffy & J. Hedley, *The Wallace Collection, A Complete Catalogue*, 2004

---

[20] 141, XIII ibid

2

The Courtyard, Cairo

The proneness to decay of all that is beautiful and perfect can, as we know, give rise to two different impulses in the mind. The one leads to the aching despondency felt by the young poet, while the other leads to rebellion against the fact asserted. No! it is impossible that all this loveliness of Nature and Art, of the world of our sensations and of the world outside, will really fade away into nothing.[21]

Freud is recounting a summer walk 'through a smiling countryside' in the company of 'a taciturn friend' and of a 'young but already famous poet'. The poet feels 'aching despondency'. He is 'disturbed by the thought that all this beauty was fated to extinction, that it would vanish when winter came [...] All that he would otherwise have loved and admired seemed to him to be shorn of its worth by the transience which was its doom.' The other 'taciturn' friend is, by contrast, rebellious 'against the fact asserted.' 'No! it is impossible...'.[22]

In the twenty-first century I have been schooled (post-modern style) to embrace such transience but I look back a century to Freud,

---

[21] Sigmund Freud, 'On Transience', 305, XIV (1914 – 1916) ibid
[22] Freud, 305, XIV ibid

the third party, the 'elder' of this group of three men, for assistance in my struggle with the 'transience' of things.

> *Transience value is scarcity value in time. Limitation in the possibility of an enjoyment raises the value of the enjoyment. It was incomprehensible, I declared, that the thought of the transience of beauty should interfere with our joy in it. As regards the beauty of Nature, each time it is destroyed by winter it comes again next year, so that in relation to the length of our lives it can in fact be regarded as eternal.* [23]

Six years ago the Tate made me a print of Edwin Landseer's friend, John Frederick Lewis's shimmering painting, *Study of the Courtyard of the Coptic Patriarch's House in Cairo* (c 1864), which I have temporarily propped up at the base of my bookshelves, eight in total in an alcove between the window and a divan, which I have covered with a warm red throw and scattered with purple, blue and red cushions. I have created a little tent, which is pitched beside a courtyard. At the heart of the tent is a bed that looks uncannily akin to the analyst's couch.

In my domestic arrangements of art and furniture I have secured (for a while) the beauty I have craved at a very deep level for most of my life. My brother's epilepsy was ugly and harsh and I was forever yearning for his beautiful face to glow with health. The beauty I see in paintings is stillness achieved. Lewis's *Courtyard* is (in my mind's eye) 'transient' in that the realities of life frequently extinguish the view, but moments of vision can be recovered and will repeat themselves. At the moment of my death they will 'fade away into nothing' but the picture and my association with it will (I hope) remain in the world for someone in the future to see with new eyes.

The picture sits at the base of my bookshelves. It is not on any wall and I think of the picture as a totem and then as an icon. As a totem it remains in my studio-tent or cave as a sign of my clan and of my history, but as an icon I can carry the work with me wherever I go. This picture

---

[23] ibid

and I can define ourselves in movement, not in that permanence so many seek above all – often settling 'down' in a final resting-place well before time. Movement compasses important permanent qualities but they can be carried elsewhere. Lewis's painting shimmers in the darkness.

Half my books are in storage, waiting to be delivered. Then I shall sort through them, deciding which to keep and which to let go. Half of me is settled and the other half elsewhere. The books I hold onto will fill all the shelves and the rest will keep in the large fitted wardrobe like a promise. Freud's twenty-four volumes sit on the lowest, the eighth shelf, and Lewis's painting is propped up in front of them.

In Freud's symbolism the number eight stands for the female genitals. I prefer to think of my eight shelves standing for a woman's whole body that is bearing the weight of many male tomes. My idea stands up to Freud's clinical and diagrammatic idea of a woman's reproductive parts. The number eight turned on its side is the mathematical sign of infinity. The baptismal font is hexagonal. I do not reject Freud's idea so much as bring it into play with my own mathematical and spiritual symbols that suggest infinite possibilities, space and the re-birth of my womanly spirit. The books on my shelves have helped me to thrive but they are not fixed forever in place: some will be discarded and some will be replaced by new words. The eight shelves remain as a sign of things to come. The painting at their base has yet to be placed on a wall.

I free Freud's idea from a deadening medical diagram of female parts and, in the process, lift his words from their weighty tomes.

> *A time may indeed come when the pictures and statues which we admire today will crumble to dust, or a race of men may follow us who no longer understand the works of our poets and thinkers, or a geological epoch may even arrive when all animate life upon the earth ceases; but since the value of all this beauty and perfection is determined only by its significance for our own emotional lives, it has no need to survive us and is therefore independent of absolute duration.* [24]

---

[24] Freud, 306, ibid

Freud's own words will 'crumble to dust' and, even though they possess a great deal of generative and regenerative power, they are also far from 'perfect'. Beauty is in the eye of the beholder and the 'object' may appear less beautiful on another occasion of looking. Freud's ideas are still potent but some of his writing is dated. I wonder if he ever saw Lewis's *The Courtyard* on a visit to the Tate in the early to mid twentieth century.

The painting is a small, modest picture measuring one foot square and I have abbreviated its name (*Study of the Courtyard of the Coptic Patriarch's House in Cairo*) so as to divest the picture of its more solemn and overbearing associations and simply to be less wordy.

The Victorian painter, John Frederick Lewis, was much admired in his day and in the twenty-first century his work is beginning to regain a wider audience. I first viewed the painting at Tate Britain in May, 2006, when I was visiting with some students. *The Courtyard* was part of a temporary exhibition, *Victorian Artists in the Near East*, on show in Room 10, a small unassuming gallery which seemed that day like an anteroom or corridor between the larger rooms that hold more well established works in the Tate canon.

Most of my students passed through Room 10, barely giving the Near East display a second glance in their eagerness to see the Pre-Raphaelites and their ladies of Shallot, along with scenes from Shakespeare and Keats. I was, though, arrested by the beauty of Lewis's courtyard painting, but had little time to contemplate the picture as I was accompanying my students on a general tour of the gallery and of more well-known 'masterpieces'. I had encouraged the students to follow where their eyes, hearts and minds drew them and reluctantly resolved to return the next day when I would have more time to focus on where my own heart was drawn.

The following morning I found Room 10 empty and I looked (undisturbed) at *my* painting for a full half hour. There were other wonderful pictures in the room by more well-known painters such as David Wilkie and Edward Lear – paintings of camels and pyramids and the Sphinx – but they paled in comparison with Lewis's luminous courtyard and the animals that gathered in its hold. The painting's light dazzled me and I felt the warmth of the invisible sun overhead lighting up the scene, where people and camels, goats and ducks, cats and birds were assembled.

At first I gazed at the picture without registering its full title. I assumed the old man with a white beard, seated in the background in the company of four younger men, was simply an old man. Even when I did take in the title, I did not imagine this elder was the 'Coptic Patriarch' in question. I assumed (with some relief) the grand patriarch was elsewhere and that this glorious scene belonged only to itself and to me, its solitary viewer. The scene was both vital and sleepy: first it took my breath away and then enabled me to breathe and settle in its presence. I longed to be in that courtyard, a participant in the scene.

As I looked at my watch, I was surprised to find that I'd been absorbed and uninterrupted for such a long half hour. Suddenly a student called Bridget appeared at my side. Unbeknown to me she had returned to the Tate as I had and now wished to talk with me about a painting of clouds by John Constable in another room. She had broken into my solitude and I rebelled. 'I want to be here forever! Leave me alone!' My child-mind protested, but the adult-mind quickly reasserted herself and took stock. Then I grew excited at Bridget's appearance. I was pleased by her arrival at the same spot as myself, albeit en route to somewhere else. I went with her to look at Constable's superlative clouds, resolving to return to *The Courtyard* later. We then went for coffee and finally parted ways after almost an hour in each other's company. I had suggested she also take a look at a very grand painting, Constable's *Chain Pier, Brighton*, which my Russian grandfather, a little patriarch (being short) of Russian Orthodox faith, had owned in the late 1940s.[25] I was almost distracted by thoughts of my grandfather and the large collection of works by John Constable and others, which he had once possessed, but my desire to dwell on Lewis's picture prevailed. I did not mention the

---

[25] **See Chapter 10**

provenance of *Chain Pier, Brighton* to Bridget, hoping that she would view the painting for herself.

It was 11.45am and the gallery was filling but Room 10 was still empty, apart from an occasional visitor glancing at the paintings before moving on. I found myself alone again in the Near East room, *my* room, half expecting that *The Courtyard* might have disappeared, but there it was and rendered more beautiful after the time I'd spent with Bridget, as if it were a field of vision that had lain fallow and was awaiting my return to continue the work of fruitful engagement. 'Limitation in the possibility of an enjoyment raises the value of the enjoyment' .[26] I spent another half hour pleasurably taking in the picture.

A few weeks later the Tate made me the print and I had it framed in moss green with a hint of gold, which brings out its lyrical, musical qualities – the kind you find in the music of Claude Debussy or Maurice Ravel or that of a more recent composer such as the late Toru Takemitsu, whose touch is light as air and wondrous with the merest of suggestions. The camels, goats and ducks, the cats and birds, the people – they rest and feed, sleep and play beside a small pond beneath a large tree that leans over into the courtyard from the right hand side of the scene.

I can see Lewis's picture in the corner of my eye resting on the floor against the lowest of my eight bookshelves. I can see Freud's volumes, with some gaps as a few volumes are scattered higgledy-piggledy on the floor whilst some are sitting on my work station as I write. The books that I inherited have been on the cusp of becoming a shrine, but at last I have been able to treat them more casually in my random readings, coming upon a wise word, a bon mot, as if by accident as I leaf through the pages. I can feel a more domestic affection for my father's edition of Freud, which renders the books less lofty. I can thank my father for his legacy without feeling overly beholden to him. This is straightforward. A daughter is thanking her father for his gift.

Ah, now I realise the 'patriarch' in *The Courtyard is* in the picture. He is the old man with a beard sitting against the wall. He is very,

---

[26] Freud, 305, ibid

very old and you might barely make him out if his presence was not made apparent in the 'Coptic Patriarch' of Lewis's cumbersome title. Had he not died in 1990, aged sixty-nine, my father would have been ninety-three years old today. *There* he is in the picture wearing a beard he never owned in life. The beard confers an authority my father did not own, apart from at very transient moments. He was always so tentative at home, as if he were forever keeping his thoughts to himself. Colleagues of his have told me he was authoritative and inspiring in his work as a psychiatrist and as a pioneer of group analytic therapy. I wish I could have seen him in action, his patients gathered together in a circle, like children at their Freudian father's feet.

I keep finding the tall tree at a tilt in *The Courtyard* particularly arresting. Its long, slim trunk seems slightly weighed down by the leafier boughs at the top. The tree looks like a protective parent (male or female) making sure the children are safe and sound. The courtyard pond beneath the tree is rectangular and in the foreground. Only half of the pond can be seen in the picture.

Beside the men and the patriarch in the background there is a column supporting the upper storeys of the large house. The lattice windows screen invisible occupants inside, apart from one woman gazing out from a lower window. You cannot see how tall the house is – the eye travels up the tree into its boughs but any upper storeys, the sky and the sun lighting the courtyard, are not in view. There are some birds that look like more delicate relations of a London pigeon, sitting on the branches of the tree or in mid-air flight, and near the centre of the picture a white dove hovers. I find myself at peace.

This is surely an immaculate conception in the mind's eye. The patriarch and the men's actual reproductive power remain in the background and the sun, as a sign of male potency, is out of sight. The picture is a celebration of feminine sensibility and flourishing. Freud might have interpreted the courtyard space as a 'uterus' [27] with the patriarch holding the 'key' (a symbol of male penetration) to the

---

[27] Freud, 'Symbolism in Dreams', 156, XV ibid

house.[28] But I am a woman looking in the present. I hold my own key to the painting. I respect the patriarch but stand in my own light. A white dove hovers in the atmosphere.

The Courtyard is in oils on wood and the effect is much lighter and more delicate than in works by the Pre-Raphaelite painters who were Lewis's peers. The gathering of animals and people seems very natural. The surface of the painting, and in my print, is silky and catches the sunlight (even at the base of my eight shelves) at midday. The picture sits beside a golden urn made of light brass decorated with delicate green trees and in their midst serpents that seem at ease with the fruit – less tempted than tamed. I picked up the urn in a shop on Clapham High Street several years ago.

I was and am still mourning the loss of my father. I cling to his memory, to the lost 'object' of my intense love for him. The work of grieving and of recollection continues, but the mourning grows lighter as years pass. I and my two much younger siblings (Robert and Elizabeth) scattered my father's ashes from a very un-decorous urn after his death in 1990. That was in the spring of 1991. The ashes were in an ugly plastic cream container and the scattering in the woods at the foot of Leith Hill tower in Surrey became farcical. We laughed and cried as our father's ashes blew back in our faces and over our clothes that windy day. We were spattered from top to toe and our father would surely have joined in our laughter. Laughter was my father's gift. He could be overly ponderous in his reverential adherence to Freud, but his enjoyment of schoolboy, P.G. Wodehouse-style jokes always came to me as a relief. Freud quotes Herbert Spencer's 'The Physiology of Laughter' in *Jokes and their Relation to the Unconscious*:

> *Laughter naturally results only when consciousness is unawares transferred from great things to small – only when there is what we may call a descending incongruity.* [29]

---

[28] Ibid, 158

[29] Freud, 'The Motive of Jokes – Jokes as a Social Process', 146, VIII (1905) ibid

The idea of a patriarch suggests rigidity and a lack of ordinary humour but small children, playing at his feet or in among the family's animals, may bring him down to earth. I see both lyric and gentle laughter in Lewis's painting. In the same year as we scattered my father's ashes my sister (a painter of lyrical power and delicacy) and I spent two weeks in Paris. We visited Auguste Rodin's garden and its statues several times. The statues of old men reminded me of my father and it was there at the Rodin Museum that I began the work of mourning, 'love's work' as the late philosopher, Gillian Rose, so beautifully called this labour.[30] The struggle for me has been to free mourning from the stoniness of my grief.

Elizabeth (Liz) is my only sister, younger by eleven years. Today she enjoys the sun in among the tall mountains of the Sierra Nevada for part of the year. She and her Spanish partner, Javier, with their two small boys, Oscar and Pablo, travel during the school holidays from Madrid to Andalusia, where they live in a stone house in the upper reaches of the Alpujarra mountain range. When Liz visited me a couple of years ago, she commented on the lyrical beauty of *The Courtyard* and I have since discovered that Lewis travelled to Spain in the 1830s. He was known as 'Spanish Lewis' and he stayed in Madrid, Toledo, Granada and Seville, where he studied the light, the life and the paintings.

Michael Lewis, the great grand-nephew of the painter, writes that Lewis painted mostly in watercolour, producing fifty studies of The Alhambra in Granada,[31] which I visited with my sister and her family for the first time last year. I was entranced by its beauty and the newly refurbished *Courtyard of the Lions* at the heart of this Moorish citadel, with its intricate arrangements of forts and gardens and galleries. In the centre of the *Courtyard of the Lions* there was the Fountain of Lions, an alabaster basin supported by twelve marble lions. I was reminded of Lewis's friend Landseer's bronze lions in Trafalgar Square.

---

[30] Gillian Rose, *Love's Work. A Reckoning with Life*, 1995

[31] Michael Lewis, *John Frederick Lewis*, 1978

He was late in his commission and growing more melancholic and depressed. Making the lions for an impatient and clamouring public became a burden.

These lions at the Alhambra were much more playful than Landseer's and smaller than I'd imagined, more like cubs or large cats. They looked happy, tame and noble in their eternal task. Water poured from their mouths as if they were little oracles gathered together and giving forth the wisdom of ages without too much solemnity.

They also brought to mind the lion Aslan in C.S. Lewis's *The Lion, the Witch and the Wardrobe*, published in 1950 (the year Andrew was born and two years before I arrived) and the book so many of my generation read and re-read in our childhoods. The memory of my many readings is lit up like the 'spots of time' Wordsworth imagined in his long autobiographical poem, *The Prelude*. These moments of illumination are stored in the memory and they serve to nourish and repair 'our minds'.[32] Wordsworth was having psychoanalytic thoughts well before their time.

Toward the end of *The Lion, the Witch and the Wardrobe* the great lion and patriarch, Aslan, breathes life into the statues in the courtyard of the White Witch's castle, after he has run like the wind with the sisters, Lucy and Susan, riding on his back, clinging joyfully to his mane. When I read the book, I would tumble off Aslan's back like those sisters, to find myself 'in the middle of a wide stone courtyard full of statues.' I was Lucy and alive but I was also one of the statues long before and then after my father died. In the presence of my brother, Andrew's terrible epilepsy I grew petrified. At eight years old Aslan breathed life into my frozen body. The lion appealed and still appeals to the child in me who desires nothing more or less than a good rough and tumble in relative safety. There was no 'rough and tumble' with Andrew when we were small children. He was much too ill and either sat propped up with cushions for a photograph taken by our mother

---

[32] **William Wordsworth,** *The Prelude, 1799, 1895, 1850,* **Ed. J. Wordsworth, Abrams & Gill, 1979**

or was falling over in a seizure or standing stock-still, jerking rigidly, mechanically, in the grip of petit mal. Sometimes he would jump on top of me, pressing down so hard I thought my back would break. My fear was intensified by his compelling pain and epilepsy's powerful, arresting grip.

The statues in the yard were petrified by the Witch at one flick of her wand and Aslan returned them to life with his breath. I was at the lion's side as he breathed on those dryads and rabbits, centaurs and unicorns:

> *The courtyard looked no longer like a museum; it looked more like a zoo. Creatures were running after Aslan and dancing round him till he was almost hidden in the crowd.*[33]

The *Courtyard of the Lions* in Andalusia was full to the brim that day last year on our visit. There was a happy atmosphere, with people gathering in the courtyard to see the long awaited restoration. Andalusia – Aslan – Andrew. They all come together in the same breath. I am gasping for air and then I laugh with the little Spanish lions and their wisdom.

John Frederick Lewis was captivated by the Alhambra and its lions. He was one of the foremost animal painters of his day and with Landseer he studied the animals in the Exeter Change menagerie on the Strand in London. Both painters produced works of art that have not yet proved transient. I am reminded of Freud's 'young poet' - the young man who cannot bear the idea of beauty being transient. The young man is myself. I have come late to a quieter and less ravenous appreciation of beauty. Lewis's lyrical paintings are beautiful in their light melancholy. They shimmer with a mature awareness that all will pass one day. By contrast Landseer is the 'taciturn' friend (my other, more familiar self) who is angry and protests against the idea – his hounds are after blood and his bronze lions are in a square, a courtyard

---

[33] C.S. Lewis, 155, XVI, *The Lion, The Witch and The Wardrobe: A Story for Children*, 1950

full of military heroes and their daring do. Landseer suffered for his art and depression and insanity eventually overwhelmed him. Perhaps, like Lewis, he might have fared better well away from England and the hungry, baying consumers who crowded into Trafalgar Square when the lions first appeared.

There is an extraordinary sense of balance in his childhood friend's *Courtyard*: its energies and focal points are evenly distributed and the many different elements, the animals and people, are in perfect equilibrium. Lewis apparently rented the courtyard and the house in Cairo from the patriarch in the picture.[34] There is no particular narrative depicted in the painting. The scene is a gathering and the food – the melon seeds offered to the goats and birds by two young women – nourish both feeling and thought. Any conflicts that might threaten to disrupt the surface of the picture are held in check by the solid structure of the courtyard, supported by the columns and protected by the storeys overhead – the tree at a tilt into the yard suggests that nearly falling is an essential condition of life and of flourishing.

To be forever on the cusp of falling may even prove delightful. In the present I may fall in love without being bound to stay in my Freudian father's domain and without being caught up inside the vertiginous sense of falling I experienced in the presence of Andrew's epilepsy, his seizures inexorably pointing to an early death and mine by long association. I may fall in love elsewhere.

Lewis spent ten years in Cairo between 1841 and 1851, the last three years with his wife, Marian Harper, twenty years his junior. They married in Alexandria in 1847 and lived in the patriarch's house in the old quarter of Cairo. They did not have children. When William Makepeace Thackeray visited Lewis and Marian in 1844 he was struck by the extent to which Lewis had gone 'native':

> *When he goes abroad he rides a gray horse with red housing*
> *[...] He wears a very handsome, grave costume of dark blue,*

---

[34] At Birmingham Museum & Art Gallery there is a watercolour of the same subject by Lewis, entitled *Courtyard of the Painter's House, Cairo*, 1850-1851

consisting of an embroidered jacket and gaiters, and a pair of trousers, which would make a set of dresses for an English family. His beard curls nobly over his chest, his Damascus scimitar on his thigh. His red cap gives him a vernacular and Bey-like appearance [...] I was anxious to know what were the particular excitements of Eastern life, which detained J., who is a town-bred man, from his natural pleasures and occupations in London; where his family don't hear from him, where his room is still kept ready at home, and his name is on the list of his club; [...] London, a razor, your sister to make tea, a pair of moderate Christian breeches in lieu of those enormous Turkish shulwars, are vastly more convenient in the long run. [35]

Thackeray recounts that Lewis was living like a 'languid Lotus-eater, dreamy and hazy and tobaccofied'. I can laugh at and with Lewis's patriarchal pretensions.

During the ten years Lewis and Marian were in Cairo the painter was silent in that Lewis put no paintings up for sale. He was busy immersing himself in the minutiae of Egyptian life and sketched a range of 'oriental' subjects – street life, bazaars, souks, harems, courtyards and animals. I love that ten year silence – a period that was fertile with the colours and scents of Cairo, fertile with the sunlight and shade of a distant land. Lewis was in Cairo well before travelling to the Near East had become fashionable. Michael Lewis writes of this decade being a period of almost secret work. On Lewis's return to England in 1851 the paintings of Egyptian life came thick and fast, belying the laziness Thackeray imagined was his friend's condition.

Lewis became eminently respectable after those ten years. He was appointed a Royal Academician, which placed him within the inner circles of the London art world, and moved with Marian to a very English address, *The Holme* at Walton-on-Thames in Surrey. I grew up in Surrey at *Holmwood House* and now in this writer's studio in a London village I return to the trees and green of my home county.

---

[35] W.M. Thackeray, *Notes of a Journey from Cornhill to Cairo*, 1846

Much has lain fallow in my mind but at this moment my words might be arriving at a point of fruition.

The painter spent his final days beside a lush inland stretch of the river and died in the summer of 1876. I like to think he let go of life beside that English river with ideas of the East filtering through the lattice-work of his fine imagination. In his last days did he dream of the stone lions at the Alhambra? Carmen Tienza, the restorer of the *Courtyard of Lions*, is said to have remarked at the re-opening: 'I recognise them with my eyes closed, like I would my children.' [36] Like the children Lewis and Marian did not have. Like the children I did not bear. They are my kindred spirits.

I visited the Near East room at the Tate several times in 2006 and then one day *The Courtyard* had gone. The exhibition had disappeared and in its place there was a display of paintings by William Hogarth. Rambunctious, satirical Englishness had filled that modest space and there was little room for lyrical oriental beauty and its light. Here were roast beef and ruddy complexions: the delicate people and animals in the courtyard had faded from view.

I felt bereft. *My* picture, *my* child, had disappeared but then earlier this year I was delighted to find it had reappeared in Tate Britain's recent re-hang of the gallery's permanent collection, *The BP Walk through British Art*. *The Courtyard* had made it into the Tate canon and the walk through the centuries. My picture has been lost and found.

I had forgotten the picture's large frame of burnished gold, which is not so much ornate as intricately woven with subtle flowers and fruit. There is a frame within a frame, a narrow inner band decorated with what looks like four-leaved clovers holding (as if by good fortune) the picture in place.

The sight of the two young women by the pond was arresting. One stood with a bowl in her left hand, from which she was feeding the birds, whilst the other sat close to the edge of the ornamental pond. The latter wore a red turban, a silk turquoise blouse and a full,

---

[36] Quoted by Mauricio Vicent, 'New tales from the Alhambra', *El Pais*, 24.7.2012

rust coloured skirt. There was a large melon sliced open at her feet and she too was feeding the birds that surrounded her. Close by there were two goats. A little springboard jutted out into the pond and a solitary duck was waddling along it, her back to the water.

The women seem absorbed, sleepy in their work and (in retrospect I see) the springboard has become a playful idea in their midst. The solitary duck was pretty and plump. Our little life is rounded in a sleep – Prospero's words at the conclusion of Shakespeare's *The Tempest*. There is magic at the heart of the patriarch's domain and in the hearts of small creatures. I am Miranda, my father's daughter. I long to stay in his courtyard but desire to be more at liberty outside. I am the heir to his beloved Freudian estate and in my studio I am bringing it into play and into my reality.

Are the two young women sisters? Liz and I sometimes fed the ducks at the pond in Walton on the Hill, a mile away from the Surrey village where we lived. The pond was a quiet place and possessed the quality of a still life picture. This picture is small and beautiful and never sublime. Freud, a man of his time, may well have passed by Lewis's *Courtyard* without giving it a second glance. It may have proved too small, too undisturbed, for an imagination that was full of ideas of the sublime ('what is more interesting, more sublime and even more abstract are only special cases [...] of what is larger.'[37]). My father's mind was similarly engaged with 'sublime' ideas.

I am a small child again in a den, a cubbyhole beneath the stairs on the mezzanine floor of my family's large Victorian house, *Holmwood*. I am dressing myself as a gypsy and then I emerge in a turquoise skirt patterned with bright daisies, gold at their centre. I wear a small white blouse, sleeveless and edged with turquoise. The skirt is one you can whirl around in and the blouse has a light pattern of little children. My mother kindly gave me the blouse last year, when I mentioned this 'spot in time'. She had kept the shirt wonderfully laundered and fresh. The lilac, orange and blue embroidery, beautifully stitched in silk, are

---

[37] Freud, 'Jokes and the Species of the Comic', 198, VIII (1905) ibid

clear as day. For all my and her eternal wandering away, my mother had preserved this emblem of my early childhood.

After climbing out of the den beneath the stairs I stand still. My feet are bare. I am on the mezzanine floor carpeted in light blue. A small black cat, Tiny (at the age of nine I chose her name), mews and brushes against my legs, her back arcing in pleasure. I emerge from the den again and again in my present day reveries and stand there contemplating the three directions that open up in front of me – the first route is up a short flight of stairs facing me, that led to my parents' bedroom; the next is down the longer stairs descending to the hallway of our comfortable Surrey villa. In the nick of time I remember the third way, which is to take the small flight of stairs behind me, arriving at my bedroom in a spacious corner of the house – a medium sized room with a window that looks out onto the two-tiered garden, the lower lawn divided by two grassy banks from an upper stretch of long, uncut grass that is full of wild flowers on summer days.

I am relieved to climb that third flight of stairs to my bedroom where Tiny's mother, a tabby cat I named Kitty, stands like a sentinel in the open door. The number three signifies the child and not Freud's male at this juncture. The twenty-four volumes can barely be seen in the darkness of the drawing-room on my father's shelves downstairs.

I look up from the past and into my day. *The Courtyard* is still there next to the gold urn at the base of my shelves and alongside the small sculpture of a giraffe and her calf, happily rhyming with laughter. A single wooden elephant stands on the fawn carpet in the middle of this arrangement. A little patriarch, he guards these makeshift properties in one corner of my room. He never forgets. The light gold curtains almost touch the floor, screening the studio from a road that can be busy with traffic at times. I stay in my studio-tent for the time being. In this long moment of writing and gathering strength I do not look further than this.

My next picture is one of sweet estrangement and melancholy.

SOURCES

Michael Lewis, *John Frederick Lewis*, 1978

W.M. Thackeray, *Notes of a Journey from Cornhill to Cairo*, 1846

Mauricio Vicent, 'New Tales from the Alhambra', *El Pais*, 24 July 2012

3

An English Wood

I must confess that I am not at all partial to the fabrication of Weltanschauungen. Such activities may be left to philosophers, who avowedly find it impossible to make their journey through life without a Baedeker of that kind to give them information on every subject.

[...] We know well enough how little light science has so far been able to throw on the problems that surround us. But however much ado the philosophers may make, they cannot alter the situation. Only patient, persevering research, in which everything is subordinated to the one requirement of certainty, can gradually bring about a change. The benighted traveller may sing aloud in the dark to deny his own fears; but, for all that, he will not see an inch further beyond his nose.[38]

I find Freud's words comforting and humble. They come at the end of Chapter 1, 'Inhibitions, Symptoms & Anxiety' (1926) in which Freud rejects a 'psycho-analytic *Weltanschauung*' that lays too much stress 'on the weakness of the ego' by contrast with the strength of the id and the

---

[38] Freud, 'Inhibitions, Symptoms & Anxiety', 96, XX (1925 – 1926) ibid

superego,[39] establishing, he implies, a knowing philosophical narcissism that feels superior to the ongoing work of painstaking scientific research into the mind's workings. In his later introductory lecture, 'The Question of a Weltanschauung' (1932/3), Freud writes that psychoanalysis must accept that as a 'specialist science' it cannot construct a Weltanschauung of its own but must accept 'the scientific one'. [40]

In that Keatsian 'den' of my imagination from which a small girl (who is myself) keeps emerging in my mind today, I was (like Freud's philosophers) 'singing in the dark' in denial of fear. I rarely saw beyond 'my own nose' in the immense fear of my brother's seizures and in an unconscious fear of the strength of my own chaotic feelings. Any sense I possessed of a 'Weltanschauung' I associated with my father, a psychiatrist and a scientist, who was full of abstractions that had him gazing into the distance and never into my eyes that followed his every move. I loved with a passion his eternally preoccupied expression. His interest in the mind gave me hope (from an early age) for a cure of Andrew's epilepsy (and later of my own long depression) and yet I felt forever excluded from that 'higher world' in which my father seemed to feel most at home.

As I grew I saw my father increasingly little. He was up to his eyes in his work at Horton hospital in Epsom and with his analysis, psychoanalytic training and directorship of the Paddington Day Hospital in London. On his return late in the evening on the train that rumbled to a halt just a few hundred yards away from our house, I listened for the front door opening when I was tucked up in bed. I would take deep breaths imagining the spot-lit places in London from which my father had returned to our Surrey village. I longed to share his preoccupation but he rarely gave me that opportunity.

An only child, my father was not at ease with children. He could be funny, telling silly jokes which had all of us rolling around in laughter, but he did not reach out to his offspring or seek to understand them

---

[39] Ibid, 95

[40] Freud, 'The Question of a Weltanschauung', 158, XXII (1932 – 1936) ibid

as children. As his eldest daughter, I realise that I was from an early age dangerously in love with my father and this lack of interest hurt me very deeply. In retrospect I can see that I felt abandoned and forsaken but never gave up the attempt to attract his real attention. I kept on trying, with increasing sophistication as I grew older, to understand my father's mind.

I developed my own brand of 'Weltanschauung': my father was my world and I believed in him and his world view. Thankfully an idea of the science of psychoanalysis was part of this view and it would eventually enable me to research and analyse this long and very wearying, if on many counts sustaining, attachment to my father. To be in love with one's father is to feel out of one's depth and very alone. When my father died I felt more beleaguered than I could have possibly imagined. I looked to a wider world I barely knew for solutions to my pain.

I began, whilst he was dying, my postdoctoral research of Victorian poetry. Alfred Tennyson wrote, 'I hold it true whate'er befall/I hold it when I sorrow most/'Tis better to have loved and lost/Than never to have loved at all.' Tennyson took nearly twenty years to mourn the death of his friend, Arthur Hallam, and to write his long poem, 'In Memoriam' (1850). It has taken me two decades to let go and fall out of love with my long deceased father. Lyric poetry, its solitary voice, is invariably mourning the perpetual loss that is life itself and the forms it takes. I looked to poetry for answers when my father died. I reached out (again like Freud's philosophers) for a 'Baedeker' of literature, scanning its timetables and destinations, the coming and going of trains of thought and emotion.

The formal requirements and rigours of postdoctoral research would carry me away, though, from a closer look at my father's 'books'. The volumes of Freud, my paternal inheritance, rarely enticed me to open their pages back then. I experienced the books as talismanic but distant and felt at a loss in their presence whilst still being in love with them as a sign of my late father. Today I am engaging with these books as a much more 'real' presence in my life and only yesterday

I held the pages close to my face to gauge the scent of my father returning me to the past.

In the immediate aftermath of his death, though, when loss was searing and insoluble, the research into my psychic pain involved turning to pictures and their quiet verities.

In the early 1990s, not long after my father died, I came upon a small square card picturing a zebra in an antiques shop off Battersea Bridge Road on the south side of the Thames. I still have the card which I found in a bundle of cards in amongst many other bundles inside my eighteenth-century seafarer's chest. The old pine chest has travelled with me for about twenty-five years and only last week I delved into its hoardings, as if into my mind, to find the picture of the zebra.

The Zebra is in oils on canvas signed with the initials, RG, English Naive School, c 1790-1830, but I have not been able to trace the painting's whereabouts. The person who sold me the card at the time said the picture was the work of an unknown itinerant painter, who had probably drawn the animal from hearsay many years after England's first zebra arrived at Southampton docks on board the HMS Terpsichore in 1762. I like to think my seafarer's chest arrived with her on the same Terpsichore, rattling in the hold where the zebra was stabled. She was a present for Queen Charlotte from the governor of the Cape of Good Hope and was placed in the Royal Menagerie at Buckingham House (Palace).

The idea of the zebra's unknown origins, her form pictured from hearsay by a 'benighted traveller'[41] of Freud's imagination perhaps, drew me into the world of the painting. I was in the dark when it came to understanding the loss of the homeland that was my father. In that darkness I did not know myself and could only hazard guesses as to the origins of such excessive grief. The seafarer's chest then became a kind of Pandora's box, its lid firmly closed for the duration of my voyage or the journey of life itself.

I recently contacted Robert Young, the owner of the antiques shop, and he emailed me from the south of France:

---

[41] See p. 47

*We sold the picture to a private English collection soon
after purchasing it in the early nineties. Sadly it was stolen
a few years later along with some important Lowry paintings.
Sometime after that they were recovered by the police and
eventually the insurance loss adjusters put it up for auction.
Sadly we underbid it. We may have the name of the purchaser
or at least contact details of the auctioneers.*

Her image found a hold, though, safe inside my seafarer's chest. I
am waiting for Robert Young to return from France and perhaps have
some news of *my* zebra. Is he looking for her in sunnier climes?[42] Lowry
and the itinerant artist have much in common in that they are painted
with a 'naive' eye. Lowry's paintings, though, are full of little, rather
unappealing people in teeming communities, whereas the itinerant
artist's zebra speaks to and with me alone.

The fact that the picture was stolen reminds me of the stolen
looks I was forever taking of my father. He has been in the corner of
my eye forever and a day. In repeated attempts to detach myself
from him when he was alive, I would find myself stealing back into his
home under cover of the dark, often on a last train from wherever I
was lodging at the time, ashamed of my failure to connect in the world
outside. I became a stranger to myself in that I could only imagine
being with my father and that meant being forever abandoned by his
very private preoccupations. This felt as if there was nothing left, even
though there was a girl waiting somewhere in the wings to come alive.
This girl was full to the brim with desire and curiosity but she did not
know it till now.

When I came upon the naive picture of the zebra my first reaction
was to smile with delight.

*The effect produced by the naive is irresistible, and seems
simple to understand.*[43]

---

[42] Robert Young recently (2015) told me that the ownership of *The Zebra* is
still unknown

[43] Freud, 'Jokes and the Species of the Comic', 182, VIII (1905) ibid

In *Jokes and Their Relation to the Unconscious* (1905) Freud associates the pleasure experienced when being surprised by 'the naive' (which is akin to the joke but the naive effect is found and not made) with the lifting of 'internal inhibition'.[44] Something about the little zebra tickled me. She is 'simple to understand'. She is black and white. The animal was female and I found the sight of her standing there, stock-still, beneath a small tree on an expanse of green, blue skies overhead, comical and also reassuring.

At the time of buying her image I had begun my doctoral research and was attending 'high theory' seminars on Jacques Derrida, Helene Cixous and others. I found the theory interesting but disliked the lofty, arch tone of the writers. The works we discussed were rarefied, densely textual and far removed from flesh and blood. The writing and discussion were inhibited by irony and knowingness and a high, overdeveloped degree of 'Weltanschauungen'.

The little zebra simply stood there, arresting me in my philosophical tracks, as if to say, 'I am here not elsewhere. I may not know where on earth I am but at least my four hooves are touching the ground.' She cut to the quick of the theoretical vanity of philosophers. The picture of her was a far cry from the reality of a zebra's living form, but she brought tears to my eyes like a gentle joke. In her presence I became less intellectually inhibited. I think my father would have found her rather crude and outlandish. In retrospect the zebra seems to be an idea of the lengths the child in me would go in order to attract my father's attention. If simply being his daughter was not enough, then I would play the simpleton and make him laugh at my naivety. I could make myself interesting to him, like a strange and curious case study.

Of course, in this contrivance and the deep inhibition experienced by a daughter in love with her father, I could not be truly naive.

It is a condition for the naive's producing its effect that we should know that the person concerned does not possess

---

[44] Ibid, 185

the inhibition; otherwise we call him not naive but impudent.
We do not laugh at him but are indignant at him.[45]

I do laugh, though, and with 'her' not him, and then close on the heels of the comic, I begin to cry at her predicament. To be 'impudent' is to be without shame. The word derives from the same root as the female sex. Pudenda are (by definition) ashamed.

I have felt deeply ashamed of the implications of this love but to be in love with one's father does not have to mean that you want to go to bed with him. I have resisted this idea in my psychoanalytic treatment and in an overly sexualised culture. To be in love with one's father does, though, involve a great deal of shame and denial. In my twenties and thirties I went out of my way to 'shame' myself sexually, promiscuously, punishing myself for the passion I harboured for my father and punishing him for his lack of attentiveness to his troubled daughter. His inattention could only exacerbate the impossible love I felt for him. Such love is destined to go nowhere. A sexual relationship is not desired but a relationship with someone in the world outside is forbidden by and to the devoted daughter.

The child resorts to drastic measures. Ha, ha! I laugh. Like the little zebra I am here to stay, whether you like it or not. I will make you see me. You will give me your full fatherly attention.

You will rescue me from the crude clutches of a world that makes me (as I make myself) its object.

Looking at the picture today, over twenty years later, I find the little zebra's naivety off-putting. I do not laugh or cry. I feel empty. I am struck by the creature's unutterable blankness and sense of dislocation. Her attempt to attract the eye is embarrassing. The figure is almost batting her eyelids at a void and her ears are like sticks of seaside rock that might be broken off peremptorily and without consideration. The tree's branches and leaves are like bits of cut out jigsaw pieces, as if her image was already broken up, manufactured. The most compelling,

---

[45] Ibid, 182

and more real, feature of the painting is the sturdy body of the zebra, but the legs that support it, like the ears that surely cannot hear, are brittle. She stands by the tree against a backdrop of English green fields, the hedges sharply drawn to denote the enclosed land. She has no idea where she is and even the itinerant painter could only imagine her from hearsay.

When my father died I became the zebra. My despair was black and white. It was extreme and extremely cut off and cut up. I was angry. Very angry. Anger isolated me from truer, more sustaining connections with others. I grew rigid and brittle in my despair. I batted my eyelids furiously, promiscuously.

The zebra was much more lyrically and realistically painted by George Stubbs and exhibited in 1763, just a year after she had arrived in England. When I first saw Stubbs's painting in January 2008, fifteen or so years after seeing the naive little zebra, I was feeling much more buoyant and hopeful. Stubbs's zebra was on display in an exhibition, *An American's Passion for British Art: Paul Mellon's Legacy*, in the Sackler suite of galleries at the Royal Academy. When the zebra (without her mate who died on board the HMS Terpsichore) had (on arrival in England) been placed in the Royal Menagerie, she was surrounded by foreigners come to see the strange animal, closely guarded by a sentinel to keep the crowds at bay. In the Sackler Wing she was again being looked at by strangers but here she was in pretty good, generally respectful company.

Michael Glover wrote about Stubbs's *Zebra* (1763) in *The Independent* (19.4.2013):

> It was kept in the menagerie at Buckingham House (Palace), companioned by an elephant, and later on transferred to the Tower of London [menagerie].

> [...] Stubbs has observed it quite soberly, with great and loving care, and he would have been delighted and surprised to see how much it differed from his beloved horses – that oh so fondleable dewlap beneath its neck, for example, and the

*way the ears point backwards and not forwards. In fact, the
care is so great that we know exactly to which sub-species of
zebra this animal belongs. It is a Cape mountain zebra, the
smallest of its kind.*

*[...] The animal is sensational in part because it seems to be
entirely at ease, utterly becalmed, as a thing to be looked
at. It has no natural place here in this English landscape, and
yet is here all the same [...] Its wildness causes us to reflect
upon the fact that it does not look especially wild, that Stubbs
himself, being inclined towards the soberly anatomical, has not
invested it with emotion of the kind that we might see had this
been painted by, say, Gericault in the following century. There
is no whiff of Romanticism about what Stubbs has done here.*[46]

How careful Stubbs was to record the zebra in all her anatomical detail,
like a perceptive analyst studying his patient and taking her in, even if
he has a way to go in terms of understanding her predicament. She
is being sent to the Tower after all! The zebra's keynote and reality
is her sadness in this poetic, but imprisoning, English setting.   She
does not stand in 'sublime' territory but surely we *are* (in disagreement
with Michael Glover) in a Romantic bower with William and Dorothy
Wordsworth peeking out from behind a tree at this strange 'solitary'
animal that has wandered into their and our view. They are hoping
that their rather wayward and excessively talkative friend, Samuel Taylor
Coleridge, does not stumble on the scene, his 'ancient mariner' in
tow to give the zebra his bright eye before perhaps felling her like the
albatross, making sure of his story in advance of hers – in advance of her
getting a word in. She will need to be wary of his deceptively stumbling
presence. She rather likes the look of William and Dorothy (are they
siblings or lovers?). Maybe they will invite her to stay at Grasmere.

The zebra has her own tale to tell and is beginning to gain
confidence in this relatively safe house of art.

---

[46] Michael Glover, 'Great Works: Zebra (1762-3) by George Stubbs', 19.4.2013

I walked through the Sackler suite, those special sequestered rooms at the top of the Royal Academy, and found Stubbs's *Zebra* in among the Romantic paintings of John Constable and J.M.W. Turner (the Wordsworth and Coleridge of British Romantic painting) amongst others. In such elevated English company she was strange as strange can be. There she was – a new arrival from the South African plains standing in silence beside a beautiful *Cloud Study* by Constable, his clouds sharing the sky with just a few birds, their wings skimming the blue, white and purple of the clouds.

I caught my breath. Paul Mellon had exquisite taste. I read on the caption that *Zebra* is on permanent display at the Yale Center for British Art, which holds the Paul Mellon collection. The zebra has found a stable in the United States at New Haven, Connecticut, as if that aptly named place knew she was coming. She has certainly been getting around.

The zebra's small form is very clear. I marvel at the soft dewlap on the underside of her neck (without wishing to 'fondle' it) and at the small hooves, which have evolved so that the mountain zebra can become sure-footed among the hills and mountains. Her skin is black and slightly chestnut-white. The leaves of the trees in the English wood, that holds her to its heart, are soft, and the thin trunks warmed by the light filtering through.

The quietness of the scene reminds me of the animals in some of Thomas Hardy's poems: the fallow deer looking in through the 'curtain-chink' of a lonely house, 'four-footed, tiptoe'; the oxen who kneel in 'their strawy pen' on Christmas Eve with Hardy 'hoping it might be so'; the 'wide-eyed' black cat who arrives at the poet's door in the snow, the poet taking her in. Like Stubbs's zebra these gentle poems are touching in their melancholy.[47] I am the animal on the outside of my therapist's room and then I am on the inside looking out. I am an English deer and no longer black and white in my grief and despair.

---

[47] Thomas Hardy, 'The Fallow Deer at the Lonely House'; 'The Oxen'; 'Snow in the Suburbs' in *Selected Poetry*, 1996

Is the zebra in the Stubbs painting recalling with her senses the journey in the dark hold of the HMS Terpsichore? The name of the ship is from Greek myth and translates as 'delight in dancing'. Terpischore was one of the nine Muses, who presided over dance. Maybe there was wild, Dionysian dancing on board, with fife and drum being played with energy and abandon, the violence and pleasures of the id breaking through and held in check by the Muse (or a strong ego). Maybe there were slaves in the hold, human cargo singing rhythmically and without abandonment, to ward off despair. When the seas were rough all you could hear was groaning. Deep below decks there was a small stable where the little zebra was being fed by an African from the plains, employed to feed this special gift for Queen Charlotte. He sings the zebra lullabies in her sleep that is troubled by instinctual animal memories of her homeland.

She has no concept or idea that she is leaving Africa, her homeland, forever. Her dreams keep returning her there. Her minder calms her when the sea threatens to deluge the ship and its animals. I am moving away from my father and his memory. Where will I land? The zebra's minder is my therapist. My father was not the zebra's 'mate' who died on the Terpsichore. Such a mate in my life has never existed, could not compete with my father, the sole object of my love. Melancholy has consumed my mind. Mourning finds the world 'poor and empty' whilst 'in melancholia it is the ego itself' that experiences the poverty and emptiness after the loved one has been lost. [48] Desire that might take another object to love is internalised in the experience of melancholy. The bereft self or ego, in its inability to let go of the intense desire for the departed, feels forever abandoned and forsaken. Freud's words are helpful. Emergence from melancholy has been 'long-drawn-out and gradual'[49] and for far too many years I forsook myself, running monotonously from pillar to post in multiple failed attempts to let go of the desire for my father's (albeit preoccupied) presence, which had always, anyway, felt more like an absence.

---

[48] Freud, 'Mourning and Melancholia', 246, XIV (1914 – 1916) ibid

[49] Ibid, 256

Paul Mellon bought Stubbs's *Zebra* in 1960 at an auction in Harrods when I was eight years old. The picture was still in the artist's studio at the time of his death in 1806. It subsequently passed through the hands of a number of private owners, before reappearing in the Harrods auction of a jumble of second-hand household furniture and goods, including a washing machine. The bidding was very competitive and Mellon bought the little zebra for the princely sum of £20,000. She was, after all her travels and displacements, worth a great deal of money.

Laurie Bradbury and my godmother, Betty Bradbury, both in the same breath first drew my attention to the Stubbs painting when I showed them the card of the itinerant painter's version. Laurie (an artist, public lecturer at the Tate and also an art therapist) smiled at me, 'Have you seen the Stubbs painting, Gill? It's very fine.' A rather better painting than the naive picture, were his unspoken words. Some day you might like to have a look at the Stubbs. See what you think.

When I came upon the 'naive' zebra in the early nineties, I was very unsure of my response to any painting. I could not wait for the next exhibition on my horizon. I was in the grip of deep melancholy and art was only just beginning to provide me with an 'object' to love in the outside world. I would become a passionate 'collector' of pictures ('objects') that appealed to or touched my imagination. I was less interested in the painting's history and provenance than I was in simply making a connection with its power to delight. I was on board the Terpsichore and gambolling with the dancers in the hold, a black and white creature cutting a strange figure.

By 2008, when I saw Stubbs's zebra at the Royal Academy, my appreciation had assumed more breadth and felt more secure. I could let myself go in the presence of paintings and follow where my response took me, without fearing I was in the wrong. I could arrive at my own view with more confidence and clarity. I had felt that my father had all the answers and that somehow I never quite hit the right note. In retrospect I can realise that it was not so much a case of my 'getting it wrong' as of his being elsewhere in his mind.

The Sackler rooms at the RA comprise the relatively new Wing on the top floor, which opened in 1991. The space, for me, still feels brand-new when I am transported up to the higher floors of the building in the glass lift. Norman Foster, the architect, remodelled the old Victorian galleries with a series of top-lit barrel-vaulted spaces. The glass-walled reception space is full of light.

As you take the lift up it is breathtaking to look out and down at the art-filled spaces. When I first visited the Sackler Wing, I felt like Alice in Wonderland, but instead of falling down a rabbit hole I was being propelled upward into art to find a rather less startling and dislocated wonderland than Alice encountered. The visitors, who make it up this far, are rare creatures. They will keep the secret and the surprise of these rooms, especially of Stubbs' sweet beleaguered *Zebra*.

The feelings I experienced back then might be likened to 'mania', an escape from 'melancholy', and certainly I have often swung between over-excitement and crushing melancholic depression in my life. There was and is (for me), though, an element of pure joy as distinct from the emotion attached to a 'high'. It is important to make that distinction. Beginning to emerge from melancholy, entering into the long, drawn-out process of getting well (and wellness is always a relative condition), I continue to be surprised by joy. Too much twentieth and twenty-first-century irony and cynicism can get in the way of recognising that a simple, transparent experience of pleasure is and can be possible, desirable, necessary.

Children love zebras (I think) because they don't arrive in their growing minds with a weight of meaning. They are capable of naivety in its truest sense. A lion stands for courage, an elephant never forgets, a tiger burns bright. The zebra, though, arrives as herself. She simply is. Her stripes, even if they are black and white and obvious, also possess an enigmatical quality, which has served her well in that she has survived thus far. The black and white stripes (what could be more obvious?) can help the zebra hide in long grass (away from the hungry eyes of predators) by disrupting its outline. The stripes confuse stalkers and this effect is called motion dazzle. A group of zebras close together may appear as one large mass of stripes, making it difficult for a lion, say, to select a target. These animals are not knowing but they do know[50].

Zebras possess a great deal of stamina, giving them the ability to outpace predators. When the animal is chased, she zig-zags from side to side. She has excellent eyesight and can see in colour. She has a wide view, as her eyes are located on the side of her head, and she possesses an acute sense of hearing, smell and taste. She does not like to be harnessed, although Walter Rothschild, the shy Jewish banker and zoological collector, did manage to harness six zebras to his carriage, which he travelled in to Buckingham Palace to prove they could be tamed. Perhaps these zebras found Walter Rothschild sufficiently strange himself, with his awkwardness and speech impediment, to allow themselves to be put in the traces.

Stubbs's *Zebra* has come to a quiet standstill for the sake of art and for my sake. She was safe in the Sackler rooms, her stable for the duration of the exhibition. I could enjoy looking at her. She was distinctive in the crowd of paintings up there and does not merge in a motion dazzle. She was not in a panic. She quietens as I look at her image online long after the exhibition closed and she was transported back to her art stable in Connecticut. The quality of stillness takes hold in my mind. Together we have travelled far.

SOURCES

George Stubbs, 'Zebra' (1762-3), *Tate Gallery exhibition*, 17th October 1984 – 7th April 1985

Lindsay Rothwell, RA, 'An Introduction to the Exhibition for Teachers & Students', *An American's Passion for British Art: Paul Mellon's Legacy*, 20th October 2007 – 27 January 2008

Michael Glover, 'Great works: Zebra (1762-3) by George Stubbs', *The Independent*, 19th April 2013

Sebastian Smee, 'A royal 'Zebra' by George Stubbs', *The Boston Globe*, 25th March 2013

---

[50] My postdoctoral supervisor, Isobel Armstrong (Professor Emerita, Birkbeck College) spoke these words in a lecture on Victorian poets in the mid-1990s: 'They are not knowing, but they do know.'

4

Cezanne's Gardener

'materia' is derived from 'mater', 'mother': the material out of which anything is made is, as it were, a mother to it. This ancient view of the thing survives, therefore, in the symbolic use of wood for 'woman' or 'mother'.[51]

My eyes rest on a wooden chair that is outside in the open air and placed near a building. The chair is in a painting by Paul Cezanne, *The Gardener Vallier* (c 1906), a late work reproduced on the cover of Adrian Stokes's beautiful Faber Gallery book, *Cezanne*, published in 1947. The old man in the chair, Vallier, is at rest and his figure embodies vitality and energy contained by an inner peacefulness that has come with age. This is one of many paintings by Cezanne of his gardener, who worked for him at his home, *Les Lauves*, in Provence during the last years of the artist's life. Cezanne painted these pictures in a studio he had built for him in the summer and autumn of 1906, not long before he died in October that year at the early age of sixty-seven (two years younger than my father would be when he died, aged sixty-nine) having contracted pneumonia after he was caught in a storm when out in the fields.

---

[51] Freud, 'Symbolism in Dreams', 160, XV (1915 – 1916) ibid

I first saw the painting in 2006 at the National Gallery exhibition, *Cezanne in Britain*, the same year as I came upon John Frederick Lewis's *The Courtyard* at the Tate[52]. This painting is my idea of perfection. Everything else fell away when I first saw the picture and this happens each time I look at it again. *The Gardener Vallier* is always there, like an old friendship that is undiminished at the end of long days. He falls into place as I write. I sit at my very modern work station recalling my former therapist's chair in the upper storey of her house in East London. I never observed her chair in detail as I lay on the couch looking at the ceiling or at a small sculpture of a woman, whose face was divided, half contorted in ugly pain and the other half smiling gently, serene. I cannot remember the sculpture in any exactness. My therapist, Tricia's chair had wood arms (I think) and was firm but comfortable looking.

I am re-thinking my past from the vantage point of contemporary modernity. There has been very little time to sit at rest as my life has been uncomfortable to say the least. I do not yet possess an armchair in which I might reminisce or enjoy long, uninterrupted reveries, but I do sit in a made to measure office chair which moves with my body and has, since I bought it twelve years ago, made a significant difference to the mild osteoarthritis in my neck, which has not only been stopped in its worn tracks, but some of the cartilage has regenerated.

In 1901 Cezanne bought a plot of land in Les Lauves situated on high ground in open countryside to the north of Aix-en-Provence. Here he designed and built his last studio, a plain, well-proportioned building with a small garden. The ground floor had living quarters and the studio was on the first floor. The studio had a high ceiling and a large window facing north. Visitors commented that *The Gardener Vallier* could be seen propped up next to his more famous paintings of ample women bathers and still life pictures.

The actual Vallier was very close to Cezanne in the painter's last days, performing many roles – that of odd-job man, gardener, nurse, carer and model. In the paintings of him Vallier is depicted as a man

---

[52] **See Ch 2**

of all seasons, his clothes changing according to the time of year.

In this painting the season is summer and the neatly bearded Vallier wears a straw hat and cool sun-dappled shirt sleeves. The picture is fresh and watery, belying the oils. The summer of 1906 was unusually hot and Cezanne found the heatwave suffocating, the watery quality of the painting perhaps providing him with some visual, even bodily, relief. The colours merge into each other but they are also distinct – sky blue, grass-green and burnished gold – their tones hold and carefully compose the gardener, who is sitting on a wooden chair by the studio wall, his arms neatly folded as if in contentment. There is a half smile on Vallier's dreamy face. The slim figure may even be half asleep, on the cusp of but never quite dropping off.

> We have earlier referred to landscapes as representing the female genitals [...] Gardens are common symbols of the female genitals.

> 'Do I really live in the thick of sexual symbols?' you may ask. 'Are all the objects around me, all the clothes I put on, all the things I pick up, all of them sexual symbols and nothing else?' There is really ground enough for raising astonished questions, and, as a first one, we may enquire how we in fact come to know the meaning of these dream-symbols, upon which the dreamer himself gives us insufficient information or none at all.[53]

Freud's reply to his imagined questioner refers him to sources such as fairy tales, myths, jokes, folklore and also to language itself:

> And, speaking of wood, it is hard to understand how that material came to represent what is maternal and female. But here comparative philology may come to our help. Our German word 'Holz' seems to come from the same root as the Greek '[hule]', meaning 'stuff' 'raw material'. This seems to be an instance

---

[53] Ibid, 158

of the not uncommon event of the general name of a material eventually coming to be reserved for some particular material. Now there is an island in the Atlantic named 'Madeira'. This name was given to it by the Portuguese when they discovered it, because at that time it was covered all over with woods. For in the Portuguese language 'madeira' means 'wood'. You will notice, however, that 'madeira' is only a slightly modified form of the Latin word 'materia', which once more means 'material' in general. But 'materia' is derived from 'mater', 'mother': the material out of which anything is made is, as it were, a mother to it. This ancient view of the thing survives, therefore, in the symbolic use of wood for 'woman' or 'mother'.[54]

In light of Freud's lovely suggestions I would say, 'Thank you, but I'd prefer not so much to live in 'the thick of sexual symbols' or with a heightened, overly biological idea of the 'female genitals', as to appreciate your insightful awareness of the importance of the 'material' of the mother's body and (I would add) of her soul.' Cezanne's gardener Vallier, in this light, becomes an idea of my therapist, Tricia, my therapy mother who sits on (in my memory) in her comfortable, wood chair, remembering me, her patient of yesteryear who came and went three and then four days a week, for over a decade, to lay down my thoughts in her presence. She is an island home of many trees where my imagination and my mind took strong root and keep growing. She and her chair continue to bear fruit in my heart and soul.

Vallier's feet are green as though dewy grass were lapping the walls of Cezanne's studio and then of *my* studio as I gaze at his image on the cover of Adrian Stokes's book. He looks out of the picture at the viewer. The hat's brim hides his eyes. Cezanne remarked that the colours grew up from the roots of the world, as though signalling that nature itself were there before and would remain long after the life of the painting. Cezanne's respect for the natural world and for the Provencal landscape is profound. The gardener and the artist can

---

[54] Ibid, 160

only attempt to arrive at an affinity with the earth, barely conscious of its deep rhythms and tones. Cezanne, Vallier and I are kindred spirits who are deeply attached to the mother and her ideas. Like those men I am barely conscious of my need and desire to touch her ground, her earth and the materiality of the trees I gaze at from my studio window.

Last summer, en route to Andalusia and the stone lions of the Alhambra in Granada,[55] I visited my sister's family in Madrid. One origin of the name of the city is 'Mayrit', an Arabic name used after the Islamic conquest of the Iberian peninsula in the 8th century. This name means 'water as a tree or giver of life'. By contrast with London, a very male and phallic city in my view (its contemporary 'Shard', for example, proving my point), Madrid seems maternal and relatively at peace in herself (in spite of her current economic problems). Jesus and Nuria, the parents of my sister's partner, Javier, were gracious and generous hosts. They took me for the customary dusk stroll through the city centre, where couples (young and old) walk in freshly laundered evening clothes, arms linked, whilst children come and go in their presence. I experienced the pace of the city as slower and less 'conscious' and driven than that of London with its quick, intent movements.

Jesus has translated my book, *The Sound of Turquoise* (2009/10), into Spanish for his own pleasure. He had enjoyed reading the story of my Russian grandfather and of my more troubled past for their own sake and for my book's likeness to 'an Impressionist painting'. A labour of love, his manuscript sits in my cabinet waiting to be brought to light. I treasure Jesus's response to my words and their colours. The 'turquoise' in the title refers to the domes of the mosques my grandfather, Alexis, glimpsed as he fled Tashkent by train following the assassination of his entire family. Freud writes that 'in dreams as well as in waking life' jewels or treasure 'describe someone who is loved'.[56] Spanish readers have in particular responded to the 'turquoise', to the colours in my book. In *The Sound of Turquoise* the subject of art

---

[55] See Ch 2

[56] Ibid, 156

and its treasures are touched upon but remain in the shadows of the traumatic narrative (the story of my grandfather's trauma and of my own) that propels the book in spite of its lyrical tone. The gentilities of love and desire remain suggestions, undercurrents.

On my last day in Madrid I visited on my own the Museo Thyssen-Bornemisza, the modern art museum not far from the Prado. In my walk through the permanent collection I came upon another painting of the gardener Vallier, entitled *Portrait of a Peasant* (1905-6). In this picture Vallier sits on the same chair but against the balustrade on the terrace of Cezanne's studio. He is dressed in the blue work-clothes of the Provencal peasant and is a little bigger, more solid, than in the Tate painting. The ochre coloured parapet suggests a more secure Vallier than in the other picture, where he drifts (beautifully and lyrically) in the eye. The parapet is a clear line upon which my eye rests. The solid structure protects him from a world that was critical, even scornful of his master's achievements. The stick he leans upon gives the picture gravitas whilst Vallier himself assumes a more symbolically male presence which gently asserts itself 'in defiance of the laws of gravity'.[57]

The picture suggests the material of the mother's body and soul that hold a man in place, but there is nothing absolute or definite about this suggestion. I love the unfinished state of the Vallier paintings. To be unfinished and both known and unknown is the condition of our being in the world and in time and space. My father died from a series of strokes at the young age of sixty-nine and in these paintings I see him in the figure of Vallier growing calm and more at peace with himself. When my father began to let go of everything that might have been said, he was signalling his imminent passing away. He chose to stop eating after three years spent chair and bed-bound. He left me unfinished but relieved that he had managed to be quietly composed at the point of death.

My father's ten year analysis with Paula Heimann (close colleague of Melanie Klein) had not arrived at a satisfactory conclusion. Heimann

---

[57] Ibid, 155

was apparently very angry with my father for ending, abandoning the analysis so abruptly when there was a lot more work to be done. I always sensed, though, that the depth of the analysis kept my father going through the years of stultifying depression that followed Andrew's death and my parents' divorce. His depression grew, along with his addiction to food and alcohol and very strong sleeping pills (not prescribed today), leading to his early death from a series of strokes. He had abandoned himself to despair but finally let go of life with grace at the point when I had begun to be absorbed in my own analytic therapy.

21st September 1977

Dr. Paula Heimann,
32 Eamont Court,
Eamont Street,
London, N.W.8.

Dear Dr. Heimann,

I was distressed to hear that you were ill and may I wish you a rapid recovery.

The reason for my ringing after so many years was that I had finally reached a stage where it seemed that the results of an analysis carried out many years ago had only at this very late stage become apparent. The catalyst was in the first place the analytic process itself, but the blocking agent was a life situation which, because of the neurotic compromise involved, made any constructive use of the experience difficult, if not impossible. The neurotic compromise was, in the end, resolved and in a painful manner. Nevertheless, the sense of internal conflict and domination by compulsive forces faded out as the painful resolution became an accepted fact, and one I could live with.

I had had in mind the idea of communicating these facts to you because the ending of the analysis and our subsequent meeting were unsatisfactory and untidy.

At least I can now say that the analysis was worth while and the final result as good as could be expected in my own very disturbed personality.

I think that it would have been a mistake to go on with any further analysis, even by someone else, at the time of our last meeting, because quite simply what I needed at that stage was the actual experience of painful events in my life, which did in the end result in my achieving a much higher degree of independence and ability to stand on my own feet.

Once more, just to say I hope that you are soon restored to good health.

Yours sincerely,
(B.A.J.C. Gregory)

My father is (I think) referring to Andrew's death early in 1977 followed by my mother's leaving the family home to set up house on her own and later to institute divorce proceedings. Andrew's death from a massive brain haemorrhage and my parents' separation had both been a long time coming. Had Andrew died at an earlier date, they may either have separated then or perhaps (given time) worked out their differences, and even have begun their marriage again in the wake of the death of their desperately ill child. The family and our development as individuals had, in the presence of Andrew's debilitating and increasingly disturbing illness, been on hold for the duration of his life and, in the immediate aftermath of his death at the age of twenty-six, the breakdown of the whole family seemed inevitable. This is the fate of many families whose child is ill and disturbed beyond what is bearable (for both the ill child and their family). It has taken a very long time to pick up the pieces.[58]

This is the first time I have written about my father's letter to his analyst. I have felt that this was the most private of documents and I did not include a copy in the holding recently created by The Institute

---

[58] My book, *The Sound of Turquoise*, explores my relationship with Andrew

of Psychoanalysis. The 'neurotic compromise' he writes of in the letter seems to refer to his separation from my mother. This does not sit well with the 'facts' as I and my two younger siblings perceived them. My father was very opposed to my mother leaving and for years was very angry with her for 'deserting' him. The marriage had badly broken down for a variety of reasons and my mother's decision to leave was very painful for her. Had my mother not left, my father would (I imagine) have continued in a marriage that involved this 'neurotic compromise'. But then perhaps my father *is* suggesting that my mother enabled him to 'stand on his own feet' by leaving him. His pride must have been very hurt by her facing the reality of their situation and taking action.

My father seems to be reassuring Paula Heimann (in her illness) that her former patient is reasonably well after all and that her work has borne fruit. Like a child he does not want his 'mother' to worry about him. He wishes to 'tidy' up after him and to leave his analytic 'home' with dignity. He acknowledges that her 'child' has a 'very disturbed personality' but that he can now with more confidence mature into adult life. The letter is painful to read, given I watched my father grow more depressed by the day after my mother left. This depression is not to be confused with 'the depressive position' advocated by Melanie Klein, indicating a point at which the reality of being alive and aware of one's mortality necessarily involves the acceptance of a certain amount of depression in the daily business of getting on with one's life.

A colleague of my father's wrote to me (on my father's death in 1990) that his late friend had been 'stoic' in his life and in his illness, never revealing much about his deepest thoughts and feelings.

In the shade of the cloisters near my studio-home, my father sits on a wooden chair wearing a boater. Here today in spirit he is tranquil, like Vallier. His outline merges with that of his analyst, Paula Heimann, and with that of my analytic therapist, Tricia Bickerton. His mother, Dr. Hazel Chodak-Gregory, had been an eminent paediatrician at the Royal Free Hospital and Vice-Dean of the London School of Medicine for Women and his father a charismatic doctor, a healer who sang Russian folk songs as he worked. This slumbering spirit at my door is the spirit of healing and of psychoanalysis and its long care for her patients. My father is sitting in the arms of many women and one small, talismanic Russian man, who will appear in a later chapter[59]. My mother, whom he loved to the last even though they were immensely different, is also in his thoughts. I, the eldest daughter, watched over my father in his long illness and now I am beginning to let him go. My brother, Robert, and sister, Liz, also nursed my father as he moved toward the end of his life. We three stood around his bed after he died. He looked so calm and composed and he had not suffered. He had made his peace.

My father vanishes slowly whilst he sits there so quietly in the evening sun, until all I can see is a faint outline and then his image breaks up and floats into the trees, the 'material' all around these Dulwich Village almshouses, and disperses in the park over the way.

This is a poem I wrote after that first sight of Cezanne's Vallier seven years ago. It is in a collection entitled *In Slow Woods*, published by Rufus Books in Canada.[60] My editor, Agnes Cserhati, takes immense care in the production of her poets' books, attending to them with delicacy and forethought. They are made in Nova Scotia from specially sourced wood to save the environment. Agnes is a poetry gardener and hopes her books will endure in our increasingly perishable world.

The Gardener
(after Paul Cezanne)

An old man's reflection
in warm dappled light
a neat frame at rest
in himself –

unfinished he sits
a brush-stroke in gold

---

[59] Ch 11

[60] Gill Gregory, *In Slow Woods*, 2011

his straw hat
symmetrical

raising his eyes edged in blue.

I was here (he will say)
in the sun long ago
casting shadows.

My poem is small but its roots are deep (I hope) and its spare syllables are thankfully free of too much biographical clutter.

Last weekend I attended a day school on Russian folk songs. Ten students and our tutor (the director of the Russian Choir in London) stood in a circle and sang by ear unaccompanied. I was moved and surprised by my voice finding the notes of such ancient songs. I thought of my grandfather, Alexis, who had lived with my grandmother, Hazel, and my father (in his early childhood) in Russell Square, a stone's throw from the room where we sang in the School of Oriental & African Studies in Bloomsbury. My grandfather possessed a rich baritone voice. The evening before the day school I discovered by chance on the internet Dr. Laura Seddon's reference to my book, *The Sound of Turquoise*, in her book, *British Women Composers*.[61] She refers to my grandfather influencing the composer, Morfydd Owen, in her fascination with Russian folk music. Owen and my grandfather had been involved (prior to his marrying my grandmother, Hazel) in a passionate affair before she went on to marry the psychoanalyst, Ernest Jones. Here was more food for thought.

My father hardly ever talked of his early life. When my grandfather went bankrupt in 1949 and disclosed a second family, a 'mistress' and two children (now my friends Nicholas and Annabel) living in another 'home', he cut off from Alexis for ten years, only attempting a reconciliation a few years before my grandfather's death in the early 1960s. My father and my grandmother (who died heartbroken at the young age of sixty-six) lost everything – their comfortable home and financial security. I have

---

[61] Laura Seddon, *British Women Composers*, 2013

wondered all my life why my father chose to train as a psychiatrist and later as a psychoanalyst but he disclosed barely anything of his earlier life. This connection via my grandfather to Morfydd Owen and Ernest Jones came as a revelation and resonated as I sang Russian folk songs, which Alexis may have sung himself, at the day school.

> 25th June 2014
>
> Dear Gill,
>
> Thank you for your message. How exciting to be connected to Morfydd Owen!
>
> We are very pleased to be looking after the small but significant memorial collection of your father's papers. You and your family are welcome to visit at any time.
>
> Best wishes
>
> Joanne (Halford)
> The Institute of Psychoanalysis

Joanne's email arrived a few days after the day of Russian songs. Her excitement buoyed me up, re-establishing the connection I had made in my mind. I hoped that this connection would not be broken.

Growing up with a brother suffering from severe epilepsy meant that my life, my very being, was constantly being interrupted by the petit mal which were ever-present. Time stood still and the memory was arrested in the moment of the seizure. Remembering what came before the petit mal, making a connection between the time before and after the fits became harder and harder. I have struggled through decades to withstand, accept and understand these interruptions to a more connected sense of the world. E.M. Forster's dictum, 'Only connect', has always resonated at a deep level, but it is only in this moment of writing that I begin to realise more fully that my own disconnectedness relates very closely to my experience of Andrew's epilepsy. The seizures were enacting little deaths every hour of Andrew's and my day. Living in the wake of these little deaths has felt like a miracle that keeps being repeated.

As my brother's illness grew worse, he became more out of reach in that he began to suffer from extreme delusions such as the classic one of believing he was the messiah. One summer, in his early twenties, Andrew announced to us that he was 'taking the word to Jerusalem' and waved us farewell as he set off in his monk's habit and bare feet. He was picked up by the police and returned home after suffering a grand mal on the road to Dover. Had he arrived in Jerusalem he may have been faced by all the other would-be messiahs sadly arrived at the same point of their delusion.

A few months after the aborted visit Andrew made himself a coffin with a seat in it. He would place the coffin upright in the large attic room and sit on the strut, playing the guitar to us and beaming with dark, surreal humour. What an extraordinary imagination my brother possessed, along with such bravery in the face of adversity.

Andrew sitting in the coffin reminds me of Charles Dickens's character, Mr Chops the dwarf, who lives in a box inside a showman's house in London. He squeezes into the box when wishing to withdraw from a society that only wishes to be entertained by him. One night, exhausted, he retires to bed and dies. In making his own coffin Andrew was predicting his own early death a few years later. I have carried and entered into my brother's surreal pain and the darkness of that box he made for much of my life. I have lain down at his side and given up his ghost. After Andrew's death I opened a Pandora's box of sorrows over and over again, as if punishing and perpetually reminding the world of my loss.

Today, though, I am looking for a less fateful box to open up and explore. I look to my father's Freud for more ideas. In *The Interpretation of Dreams* he writes of house-symbolism and boxes in general as symbols of the uterus, which might also be symbolised by 'the shell of Venus' (VI, 77), the 'baby-box' (X, 95) or a container holding an embryo (IV, 154). Much has lain dormant or dead in my own metaphorical womb. I have never fallen pregnant, partly through careful use of contraception but also because I lived very much in the grips, the talons, of an eating disorder up until my mid thirties. My periods stopped for several years in my late twenties when I was bulimic and a distorted relationship to food, the absence of a more natural feeling and desire for nourishment, halted the development of embryonic potential, actually and metaphorically.

I have only ever been 'in love' with my father and this love (that can only be sterile) has inevitably stopped my heart from beating truly in the outside world. I fell in love with Freud alongside my father and have expected far too much of them both. Now that I have taken the books down from their shelves I find myself alive and blossoming in their use. I find myself halfway through writing this book and there is a great deal of life yet to be lived on its pages.

In 2012, six years after coming upon Cezanne's *The Gardener Vallier*, I made a very surprising discovery. Among the many treasures of the Tate archive I found *The Stoop Bequest*, a collection that includes the painting of Vallier by Cezanne. The Stoop in question is a man, a stranger I had not met with before. *The Gardener Vallier* is the keynote painting in the important bequest made to the Tate Gallery in 1933 by Cornelis Frank Stoop of Dordrecht, a collector on my mother's side of the family. Over the years I had heard of *The Stoop Bequest* but this was a vague, shadowy presence in the back of my mind, like food that might possibly make my mouth water or a lovely idea way, way beyond my grasp.

Although I and my family visited my uncle and aunt, Peter and Susan Stoop, on their Wiltshire farm in Ashmore, I did not associate my mother's family with art. There were pictures of farming scenes on their walls that caught my child's eye in passing, but they were not the subject of any conversation I can remember.

With great prescience and generosity, Cornelis Frank Stoop (known as Frank Stoop by his close friends, who numbered Samuel Courtauld and the Bloomsbury critic and artist, Roger Fry) bequeathed Cezanne's

The Gardener Vallier, along with thirty-eight paintings, drawings and sculptures, to the Tate in 1933. The bequest was the first significant collection of modern art to be held at the Tate.

I visited the Tate archive at Tate Britain for the first time in 2013 and among the pleasures I found was the archive itself. The *Hyman Kreitman Reading Rooms* on the lower ground floor of Tate Britain had recently been refurbished, providing a dedicated space for research and creative thinking which is accessible and free to use by anyone who makes an appointment.

Hyman Kreitman, who died aged eighty-six in 2001, was a significant benefactor of the arts. He was also a sculptor and a collector of sculptures by Barbara Hepworth, Henry Moore, Elizabeth Frink and the late Anthony Caro amongst others. His friendship with Sir Norman Reid (director of the Tate between 1964 and 1979) led to his contribution to the development of Tate Modern on the South Bank and to the funding in full of the Library, Archive and Reading Rooms, which opened in 2002. Sir Nicholas Serota, Director of Tate, writes 'This was a project that reflected Hyman's commitment to learning, and his recognition that imaginative scholarship lies at the heart of every successful museum.'[62]

On this first visit to the archive I fell in love with the relatively small space (compared, say, with the British Library at King's Cross) and the sense of the librarians and archivists enjoying their work, taking a high degree of pleasure alongside those using the facility. That is not to underestimate the very hard work everyone is engaged in. I immersed myself happily in the gentle but busy atmosphere of the place. There was a lot going on in this 'womb' below ground. I had a sense that things were being unearthed all around me, as though all us researchers were engaged in an archaeological dig.

I had ordered the files in advance and was excited when the archivist brought the first of several boxes, advising me to be careful with the documents and only to use pencil when taking notes. I lifted

---

[62] Nicholas Serota, *The Guardian,* 21.5.2001

the lid of the ur-box and to my amazement, on top of the pile of papers a treasure disclosed itself: here was a letter, pristine and fresh as if unread, addressed to Ronald Alley, Keeper of the Modern Collection, from my uncle Peter Stoop, my mother's brother-in-law.

27/4/85

Major P.F. Stoop
Ashmore Farm
Ashmore
Salisbury, Wilts.

Dear Mr Alley,

On behalf of all my family I would like to thank you and your staff for all the time and trouble you took over our visit yesterday. It was a day that the young will always remember and satisfies my own conscience that they have now seen the famous 'Stoop' collection.

Also they learnt a little about my godfather: that great-great Uncle. As most of us now have some of the 'Dutch' Family Paintings – which grandfather F.C. Stoop collected, I am not sure that we fully appreciate the 'Impressionists' and it was indeed fortunate that at least Uncle Frank had the foresight necessary to do so.

We were delighted that you were able to join us for lunch on such a happy occasion. Most families only meet in these sort of numbers for funerals!

Thank you also for providing us all with a copy of your *most* excellent 3rd Revised Edition of the Catalogue. This will give us all much avid reading and reference.

I will try to piece together a little more history about Frank Stoop which can be of use to you and your department.

Again thank you so much for all your care and trouble.

Yours sincerely
Peter Stoop[63]

I remember my uncle and aunt were not that interested in modern art.

---

[63] In the Stoop Bequest holding, Tate Archive

Uncle Frank was actually a collector of Post-Impressionist and modern art, not the work of the 'Impressionists' my uncle Peter mistook them for. He and my aunt had Old Masters on their walls, the 'Dutch family paintings' such as those of Albert Cuyp, which my uncle had inherited from his Stoop family. As landed gentry they preferred the paintings that suggested the solidity of inherited wealth and its art. They also naturally loved pictures of the countryside farms.

My aunt and uncle's Ashmore Farm was a beautiful 1920s shooting lodge in the village of Ashmore, which you arrived at after ascending Zig-Zag Hill, much to the delight of myself and my siblings. I never knew my uncle particularly well and I am very sorry he died before I came upon the Stoop bequest. My uncle's forebear, Frank Stoop, was a collector of rare taste and boldness in that he chose to buy works (by Cezanne, Picasso, Van Gogh) as yet unrecognised as valuable objects. He had believed in their potential and, if the wider world had still not recognised their quality, he and his friends, 'Sam' Courtauld and Roger Fry, would still have enjoyed and valued the pictures nonetheless.

The next document I found in the box of treasures was an obituary and review by Roger Fry published in *The Times* on the death of his friend on November 7th, 1933.

> *The death of Mr. Frank Stoop is a serious loss to a wide circle of lovers of art. His collection of modern art gave evidence of his discriminating judgment and fine taste. The collection was select rather than impressive. It contained no pictures of which the fame had been widely acknowledged; rather they gained their title by admission to so select a company. Rarely has one seen a Van Gogh to equal Mr. Stoop's example [...] Cezanne was seen in a precious and rather late work [...] No collector could have welcomed lovers of art with a more engaging and lavish hospitality than he did, and our regret at having lost a patron of art is increased by our deep sense of personal loss.* [64]

---

[64] Obituary in Stoop Bequest holding, Tate Archive

Yesterday I re-visited Cezanne's *The Gardener Vallier* at the Tate Stores in Mandela Way south of London Bridge. The Stores are part of a huge industrial complex and one of their technicians showed me around the large warehouses, opening and closing massive strong-room doors, leading me into capacious, womb-like caverns full of paintings, many in crates. I was astonished to see J.M.W. Turner's oil painting, *The Old Chain Pier, Brighton* (propped against a wall) which he painted in 1830. I also saw Mark Gertler's lovely *Portrait of a Girl* (1912) with her lilac blouse and string of red beads. A picture of modernity, she looks at her viewers quizzically, her hair swept off her face into a lilac and red spotted turban. This is a painting I saw for the first time at a recent exhibition in Dulwich Picture Gallery. Presumably 'the girl' was in the Stores en route to another destination. I wished her a safe journey.

The Gardener Vallier was at the bottom of a screen so I had to kneel down, as though in homage to this painting. He looked rather beleaguered and forlorn down there but, when I studied it closely, he came alive in the colours of the earth and the sky and the green of the land. I liked his beard especially. It was softer than I had remembered. On my way out of the Stores I met a research assistant from the Tate in the foyer and we talked about our work. He had a beard rather like that of Cezanne's gardener.

On my way home to the village I felt refreshed and absorbed by these discoveries.

SOURCES

The Stoop Bequest holding, Tate Archive

5

A Dutch Collector

Children frequently manifest a desire to exhibit. One can scarcely pass through a country village in our part of the world without meeting some child of two or three who lifts up his little shirt in front of one – in one's honour.[65]

Freud's little boy (who greets my readers in the 'Preface' and makes way for the little girl in my imagination) might be my new friend, Frank Stoop, now grown to manhood. He and I can delight in the exhibition of his paintings.

On my second visit to the Tate archive I dipped into another box and found a long article entitled *Frank Stoop's Collection* but with no author cited. On the front page there was a photograph of Frank in his later years, probably taken not long before he died, aged seventy, in 1933. He has a square face and wears a well-trimmed white moustache. Dressed in a neat, casual suit, he is leaning on a stick. There are people in the background walking toward a lighted building, which might be a summer pavilion as it looks as if the building is domed. The picture has a relaxed and hopeful appearance.

---

[65] Freud, 'Typical Dreams', 244, IV (1900) ibid

On the next page there was a picture of *The Stoop family Triptych* (1534-35) by Jan Van Scorel, a Dutch painter. The painting is of the Holy Family and Donor, Dr. Willem Stoop. Here was a long established family. I returned to the picture of Frank Stoop and he assumed a spiritual air in the light of the triptych. He also looked very human, a little melancholy and a touch tentative.

The article was illuminating. Cornelis Frank Stoop was born in 1863 in the market city of Dordrecht in Southern Holland, the seventh son of Adriaan Stoop. He had seven brothers and two sisters. The Stoop family had been distinguished merchants and bankers in Dordrecht since 1280 and, among their many enterprises, they owned a brewery that produced Oranjeboom beer. The Dutch word 'stoop' means 'a pitcher'.

In 1873 an elder brother, Frederik, left Holland to set up a stockbroking firm, Stoop & Co., in the City of London. Another brother, Adriaan, was a geologist in the Dutch East Indies, where he found signs of oil (which was only used for burning in lamps back then) and went on to set up the Dordtsche Petroleum Maatschappij, striking oil in 1888, which made a massive fortune for the family. Yet another brother, Theodor, remained as a doctor in Dordrecht, where he became the first ever social democratic mayor.

His elder brothers' achievements must have been hard acts to follow. Frank, the seventh child of ten children, was apparently a quiet man who married Bertha Keller van Hoorn, the daughter of a churchman in Dordrecht. He then joined his brother Frederik in the London stockbroking office of Stoop & Co., where he worked for the rest of his life, becoming one of the founding members of the Netherlands Chamber of Commerce in London. He and Bertha lived in a large house at 9, Hans Place, a garden square just behind the famous department store, *Harrods* (where the little zebra was recovered in the 1960 sale[66]) and there he housed his famous collection.

I discover with astonishment that Frank Stoop and his close friend, 'Sam' Courtauld, shared (along with Viscount Rothermere and the

---

[66] See Ch 3

Art Fund) in the cost of buying the celebrated *Wilton Diptych* for the National Gallery in 1929. Frank's contribution amounted to £10,000 (an enormous sum at the time).

All this information, the details of such a prosperous and active family, was at first rather overwhelming and then, as I turned the pages of the history, very welcome. I have looked to my father as my sole 'love object' and life outside my father has frequently passed me by as a result, but here I was meeting a brand new family of Dutch strangers. My father became, and I in my turn, reclusive in later years but I am now welcoming movement and possibilities in the world outside the 'cloisters' where my father in the form of Cezanne's gardener still slumbers.

Freud wrote that a lot of strangers in dreams 'always stand as the wishful contrary of 'secrecy'[67] – the secrecy desired for the intimacy required for the child's relationship to the desired 'single familiar individual'. Strangers, he states, are not interested in a child's exhibition of his nakedness before them. I have found many strangers in my dreams and in my early twenties, in flight from my father and the intensity of my love for him, I found a home among strangers in Dublin. I immersed myself for four years in a communal culture where life was to be found in gatherings – in pubs and in people's homes where folk music and song held me entranced. I kept myself to myself, though, even when surrounded by strangers in the crush of a pub. I lived in Dublin as if in a dream and Freud's words ring true.

These Dutch strangers of very recent acquaintance, though, are from my mother's side of the family so we are related. This is concrete history and I am awake in the presence of people who are actually not so strange and may prove to be good company. As I read this history Frank and his family walk, even trip across the page, one after the other bearing pictures and I am no longer tied to the ground of my father's house. I am no longer akin to the people in Plato's cave shackled to the earth and facing a wall that reflects the shadows of the world and its art passing them by. I am in Dordrecht and then I find myself standing

---

[67] Freud, 'Typical Dreams', 245 - 246, IV (1900) ibid

among a crowd in the Netherlands Chamber of Commerce in London. Like Herbert Pocket in 'the counting house' in Charles Dickens's *Great Expectations* I am 'looking about me' for opportunities that might arise. I am in Harrods with my mother in 1968, aged seventeen, and we are admiring the fashionable clothes in the newly opened *The Way In* boutique. I choose a single-breasted red woollen coat which is warming, but back then I carried around with me a sense of doom I did not, could not, understand. I looked on at the bright colours of the clothes in *The Way In* but could not believe I was really part of the scene and its clothes. Only my father existed. Whatever I chose to wear meant nothing out of doors.

In the Tate archive I found myself feeling breathless with antici-pation. 'The heart will be represented by hollow boxes or baskets.' Freud is quoting the nineteenth-century philosopher, K.A. Scherner, in his discussion of dream symbolism.[68] The box that held the Stoop his-tory and the pictures Frank collected is filling *my* heart with pleasure. In reading of the Stoops and of Frank and his pictures I am entering into a dream of belonging in wider company. This archival box was not a Pandora's box but a heart whose hollowness was filled to the brim with hopefulness.

On the next page I find a picture in colour of Cezanne's *The Gardener Vallier*, the keynote painting signalling Frank Stoop's modernity. Impressionist paintings had barely arrived in London when Frank was looking over their dreamy heads to later developments – to Paul Cezanne and the 'post-Impressionist' paintings championed by Roger Fry. Such art had not yet been welcomed by the public or by the art establishment in England.

The idea of Frank's insightful collection, and its place in the nation's memory of art, prompts me to think about the difference between the word 'memory' and the word 'recollection'. The first has its origin in the Latin *memor* which means mindful or remembering. 'Remembering' has its root in the late Latin, *rememorari*, translating as 'call to mind'.

---

[68] Freud, 'Theories of Dreaming and Its Function', 87, IV (1900) ibid

There is a summoning, an invocation, implied by the word. By contrast the word 'recollection' is a later word from the sixteenth century, its root in the Latin *recolligere*, the verb meaning to 'gather back' or literally 'to collect back' or 're-collect'. To 'collect' is an older Middle English word from the Latin *collecta*, 'gathering', the feminine past participle of *colligere* 'gather together'. The idea of recollection suggests more of an active search than is implied by 'memory'. To recollect is to return to the past and collect its images or pictures, sights and sounds, fears and feelings. Recollection keeps repeating itself, as I do on my therapist's couch. I keep remembering and forgetting and recollecting. There is some idea of purpose here – the purpose that takes me to therapy which in turn surprises me with unearthed memories or with the processes involved in forgetting.

Frank Stoop's collection of pictures becomes a gathering of thoughts and affects that move or rest in my mind – sometimes they are in the foreground and a central focus but more often they are seen in the corner of my eye on the walls of my psyche. I am not well-versed in science or in the finer details of Freud's expositions but, in my random reading of his twenty-four volumes, I use what most makes sense in my writing. Many years ago I attended a discussion led by the poet, Andrew Motion. I cannot remember the actual subject that day on the creative writing course in Devon, but I do recollect him saying he thought 'unconsciousness' might not be a bad idea when it came to writing or reading or engaging with art in general.

Freud might have agreed with Motion had he been around in our time. His General Subject Index (the twenty-fourth volume of Freud's Standard Edition) is filled with references to the 'Unconscious' which fill two and a half pages in all their suggestions and permutations. From 'absence of doubt in' to 'incestuous wishes and' to 'repression and' to 'timelessness of' to 'popular ignorance of' etc.[69] The 'unconscious' since Freud has proved to be a source of perpetual fascination as we wonder what is really going on in our minds. Andrew Motion was,

---

[69] Freud, 'Indexes and Bibliographies', XXIV ibid

though, suggesting that to be truly 'unconscious', in the Keatsian sense of 'negative capability', might allow the mind to be more creative and less neurotic. I think Freud would have been shocked to see how intensely self-conscious we have become. Even if his ideas are rejected by many today, the existence of an unconscious is taken as read by most people, even if they do not realise it. To explore the unconscious is potentially far more rewarding (if painful at times) and surprising than being caught up in self-consciousness and inhibition. Such an exploration is an unending process of engagement and re-engagement. There is no point at which one can exclaim like an overexcited and triumphant child, 'Ah, now I know everything that is going on in my mind! Now I am on top of the world! Hurrah!'

Frank (and his name derives from the medieval Latin, *francus*, free, and also denotes generosity) bought his pictures, as if instinctually, before they had been recognised by the art establishment in this country. He did not doubt their timeless qualities (both features of Freud's 'unconscious') and, even though these modern paintings would go on to be over-discussed by many as expressions of Freud's new idea of the unconscious, it was Frank's openness to their freshness and appeal that secured them for the nation. To be genuinely child-like as an adult (not to be naive but to be open to impressions as we once were as children) is to open one's heart in the re-collection of the memory of how that once felt in the midst of our beginnings.

During the 1920s the Tate (like a strict and old-fashioned parent or 'super-ego') had still not admitted works by Cezanne, even though Sir Joseph Duveen (another Dutchman) offered to provide money for a purchase. It was not until 1933 that Frank Stoop's bequest marked the painter's long-overdue entry into the Tate collection. The bequest included the first Cezannes, the first Matisses and the first Picassos ever to be housed by the Tate. These very modern children were allowed into the inner sanctum at last.

Frank and Bertha did not have children but he left generous legacies to the National Society for the Prevention of Cruelty to Children, the London Orphan School and many other charities and hospitals for children. In their absence he cherished paintings. James Bolivar Manson, former Director of the Tate, wrote an article published in *Apollo* (September, 1929) entitled *Mr Frank Stoop's Modern Pictures* in which Cezanne's painting of Vallier occupies a full page. On the front cover of Adrian Stokes's Faber book on Cezanne (1947) Vallier stands, like a sentinel, mindful of the children in his care.

Manson writes:

> *French impressionism is not definitely represented in the collection; there are no pictures by any of its masters. Mr. Stoop is more interested in the later developments. That movement had an effect similar to that of opening a gate and releasing a host of youthful spirits, and it is their adventures in this wider sphere which may be said to be represented here.*[70]

Cezanne's gardener is surely conjuring those 'youthful spirits' in his imagination as he sits there in his chair contemplating their new beginnings inside the house of art. The wise old man of the collection, he was himself unfinished, as if he had not quite settled into a vision of old age and was capable of something more as he moved toward the end of his day.

> *Mr. Stoop appears to like his Cezanne before the work is pushed to the utmost completion. [...] But Cezanne's work has this characteristic: that at whatever stage it is at, it appears to be complete. And certainly it is fascinating in its unfinished state when the method is revealed in unpretentious freshness.*
>
> *[...] With Cezanne every stage in the progress of a picture is expression, not so full nor so complete as the final stage, but sometimes even more attractive. 'The Gardener' seems to be as complete as it need be. If he had told us more*

---

[70] J.B. Manson, *Mr Frank Stoop's Modern Pictures, Apollo: A Journal of the Arts,* September 1929

psychologically about the gardener it might have been at the
cost of something of the beautiful clarity of his expression. [71]

To achieve clarity is a life's work and too much Freud can get in the way of the more unconscious expression necessary to such clarity. To be aware of our unconscious realm is, though, to be deeply indebted to Freud. Now that the 'unconscious' is a given (invariably without being understood in all the richness of the idea) we are not, in our enthusiasm, obliged to uncover everything that goes on in there, as if one only need bring unconscious desires to light for all to be resolved. To do so might leave us with very little to enjoy or play with, or to take a more natural course and at times burst gloriously into life.

Frank was angry at the Tate's intransigence and stuffy lack of appreciation for the 'youthful spirits' he wished to usher in through its portals. In February 1929 he wrote a very sharp letter to Manson about the Tate's 'discouragement [...] given to friends of Modern Art.' He even threatens to reconsider the bequest and 'leave pictures to Ryksmuseum in Amsterdam', which (as a Dutchman) would have been a very natural gift for him to make. [72] Manson's article was published later that year in September, suggesting he might have been jolted by Frank's letter into reassessing the paintings that were to comprise the Stoop bequest.

That day of my discoveries, I sat back in my chair at the archive and drew breath. What a surprising encounter (in this secluded but busy mind or womb below stairs at the Tate) with a strange but familiar man I warmed to in reading about him.

My uncle Peter's family were proud of the Old Masters, especially Albert Cuyp's paintings of Dutch farm life, which they had inherited. One of the seventeenth-century Golden Age Dutch painters, Cuyp had lived in Dordrecht, the home of the Stoop family. They probably knew the artist and were his patrons. The paintings by Cuyp on my aunt and uncle's

---

[71] ibid

[72] Letter in Stoop bequest holding, Tate Archive

walls were there in my background, sowing in me the seeds of a love of art. These very earth-bound paintings of the land were not so much on display as embedded in the fabric of my aunt and uncle's daily existence.

I do not know which specific paintings hung on their walls but yesterday I studied Cuyp's *Herdsmen with Cows* at Dulwich Picture Gallery. This beautifully composed picture of a herd at rest in a green landscape beneath a blue sky with light clouds on the point of dispersing, returned me to the rich detail of farm life at Ashmore. I loved looking at the herds of cattle grazing in the fields from the vantage point of the beautifully symmetrical two tier garden. As a child I was a natural vegetarian, but ate meat without thinking and because it was taboo not to. I flinched away from talk of the hunt (I don't remember ever being asked to participate, thank goodness) and the idea of any of the animals on the farm being killed.

I loved, though, the herds and unconsciously registered their idea which would surface decades later in a poem I wrote after Pieter Bruegel the Elder's painting *The Return of the Herd*:

The Return of the Herd

He understands their drift
implies a favour
filtered through

a close-knit dream
or pattern of arrival

the reddish lane
warm hearts
in age approved.

His autumn frames my fear
(stoic in the trees)

a rust-stained line
of living things

if I'm not deceived.

Freud writes of 'the herd instinct' as a regressive instinct. Its features include 'the lack of emotional restraint, the incapacity for moderation and delay, the inclination to exceed every limit in the expression of emotion and to work it off completely in the form of action' .[73]. I have certainly shied away from human 'herds', finding large festivals, rock concerts, demonstrations, crowds in general too prone to mass hysteria, hero or heroine worship and the abandonment of more level-headed judgement.

My idea of an animal herd, though, has usually taken the form of cattle gently grazing in fields. When I wrote 'The Return of the Herd' about fifteen years ago I did not quite understand it but liked the sound I had achieved. The journal, *Poetry Review*, under Robert Potts's editorship, published the poem, and Potts wrote to me that he liked 'The Return of the Herd' but was not sure he (like me) entirely understood it. In writing of the poem now, I think I am beginning to get its 'drift'. Freud writes, 'The fear shown by small children would seem already to be an expression of this herd instinct.' [74] The fear of being alone. My poem or 'close-knit dream' seems to invoke the 'fear' of the child whilst calming and holding it inside the poem, inside the trees, inside the herd. The adult speaker fears she is being 'deceived' whilst allowing the child in her to be held in a relatively comfortable, even beautiful, place. The 'line' of the herd and of age, the 'line' leading from childhood to adulthood is imagined and 'heard' and secured. In the process I am being 'heard'.

My 'herd' is not so much regressive as an idea of collectivity, within which the intense subjectivity of the individual may be quietened and warmed by the nuzzle of unconscious herbivores. Of course my uncle's herds of cattle were either being milked or killed for meat when they weren't grazing: many would be led to the slaughterhouse. In wild herds the animals have natural leaders and they herd for survival. My 'herd' is poetic and utopian and does not fear predators.

---

[73] Freud, 'The Herd Instinct', 117, XVIII (1920 – 1922) ibid

[74] Ibid, 118

Chapter 1: Edwin Landseer, *The Arab Tent*, 1866, The Wallace Collection

Chapter 2: John Frederick Lewis, *Study of the Courtyard of the Coptic Patriarch's House in Cairo*, c 1864, Tate Britain

Chapter 3: George Stubbs, *Zebra*, 1762-63, Yale Center for British Art, Paul Mellon Collection

Chapter 4: Paul Cezanne, *The Gardener Vallier*, c 1906, Tate Britain

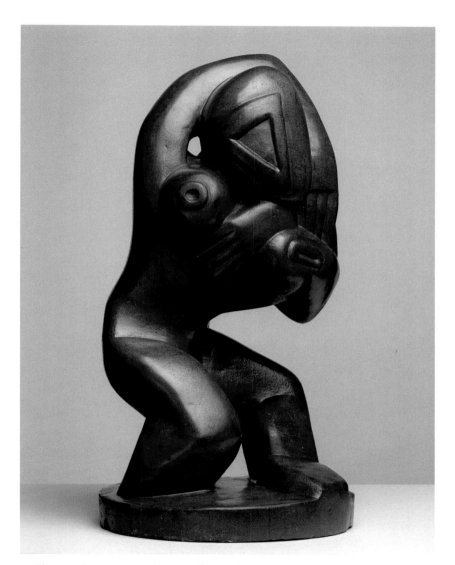

Chapter 7: Henri Gaudier-Brzeska, *Red Stone Dancer*, c 1913, Tate Britain

Chapter 8: Henri Gaudier-Brzeska, *Eland*, c.1912-13, Tate Britain

Chapter 9: Vincent Van Gogh, *The Oise at Auvers*, 1890, Tate Britain

Chapter 11: C.R.W. Nevinson, *A Studio in Montparnasse*, 1926, Tate Britain

In finding myself among paintings and in psychoanalysis I have come upon what is closest to myself. In re-reading and re-collecting the poem and its words I would like to change the last line. Instead of 'If I'm not deceived', I will insert a single word 'retrieved': 'a rust-stained line of living things/retrieved.' When I stayed on my uncle Peter Stoop's farm, collecting the warm brown eggs, I loved to run, even race out into the fields with Kim, the farm dog (a golden retriever) running ahead of us. Kim's animal spirits are now in tune with the child of the fields I once was, even if only for moments. A painting of Kim from the early sixties now hangs in the hallway of my mother's flat in a Surrey market town. When I visit I can retrieve this picture and its good memories. In discovering Frank Stoop and his collection I find a man who is a kindred spirit. We are in among the art herd, a gathering of like-minded friends in the summer pavilion I can see behind Frank's figure in the photograph. We are nice and warm.

SOURCES

The Stoop Bequest holding, Tate Archive

6

A Cezanne Picnic

Humour is not resigned; it is rebellious. It signifies not only the triumph of the ego but also of the pleasure principle, which is able here to assert itself against the unkindness of the real circumstances.[75]

I have yearned for and then succeeded in becoming one of the herd gathering in that summer pavilion of art. The more often I am invited to such gatherings, though, the more beleaguered is the self who feels excluded. The beleaguered self sits on a brown and beige checked rug her mother has taken from the boot of the car to lay down a few feet away from the main event.

My mother was and still is an artist of the makeshift meal, the picnic taken in fields near the road we travelled by, usually on our way to the West Country for holidays by the sea. We partook of the same makeshift meals on beaches in all weathers and there was hopefulness and triumph, combined with despair, in my mother's eyes, as if she were thinking about her child, Andrew, and his relentless epilepsy. She is determined that his life will be the best possible and that her family will survive the many trials and tribulations of his illness. She is

---

[75] Freud, 'Humour', 163, XXI (1927 – 1931) ibid

perhaps also recollecting a childhood trauma of her own, which she has never revealed to her immediate family. I have sensed something extremely painful , hurtful, in her background. Her light blue eyes evade any probing. 'I will not allow life to get the better of me,' they seem to reflect and challenge. 'I refuse to be beaten!' And then she smiles, a touch grimly, as though she were enjoying a joke her family will never understand.

My father sits mournfully on the rug gazing out to sea or at the horizon. He might be thinking about the impossibility of imagining any kind of bearable future for his son. Maybe he is mourning the loss of the early promise in his marriage, the growing gulf between my mother and himself, which is very common in the parents of an intractably ill child. They were also very different in many ways. My father was naturally tentative, my mother determined and purposeful. He was in love with the mind and classical music, my mother with dancing and the fields and the practicalities of family life. I always sensed that my father would give up too early on life (to die at the age of sixty-nine is to be on the cusp of getting truly old) and that my mother would continue to stare life in the face, at times menacingly (at which point I grow afraid) but for much of the time with a humour that has enabled us all to bear with pain and struggle.

My therapist, Tricia, once commented: 'Your family know how to have fun!' Yes, we did and still do, but, in Toni Morrison's words that open her wonderful and heart-breaking novel, *Sula*, 'laughter is a part of the pain'. Freud wrote of humour (as distinct from jokes) as 'a rare and precious gift'. He believed that it triumphed, for better and for worse:

> It is now time to acquaint ourselves with a few of the characteristics of humour. Like jokes and the comic, humour has something liberating about it; but it also has something of grandeur and elevation [...] The grandeur in it clearly lies in the triumph of narcissism, the victorious assertion of the ego's invulnerability. The ego refuses to be distressed by the provocations of reality, to let itself be compelled to suffer. It insists that it cannot be affected by the traumas of the external

world; it shows, in fact, that such traumas are no more than occasions for it to gain pleasure. [76]

In the face of 'reality' my father was resigned, stoical. My mother, by contrast, seemed to embody the spirit of defiance in response to the daily trauma of Andrew's illness, which she had to bear whilst my father was at work. At the age of twenty-one, when Andrew was born, she must have felt very alone with her child in a world that had little understanding of epilepsy. She grew very angry at that world and I can see my mother waving the red flag of revolution against society's indifference wherever she went. To rebel was also a way of keeping excessive pain in abeyance.

One of my mother's dictums has been to 'travel light' – whether it be on a holiday, going to work or in one's own home. Like my mother, I have not allowed the dust to gather, jettisoning possessions at every turn up until the past decade when I have begun to slow down and take my bearings. I still love her idea, though, and bear it in mind as I go about my days. My mother sometimes reminds me of Robert Louis Stevenson.

I travel not to go anywhere, but to go. I travel for travel's sake. The great affair is to move; to feel the needs and hitches of our life more nearly; to come down off this feather-bed of civilisation. [77]

Whenever travelling anywhere with my mother I have felt we were together embarked on a great and humorous adventure, even if it was only to the village shops round the corner from where we lived in The Avenue, and I have never been able to reconcile my feelings of excitement with an overwhelming sense of our being beleaguered beyond reason. My mother seemed forever elsewhere in her mind but very much in control and driven by an overriding desire that 'the

---

[76] Ibid 162

[77] From Sidney Colvin's dedication to R.L. Stevenson, *Travels with a Donkey in the Cevennes*, 1879

pleasure principle' would win out. There was and is, of course, a great deal of 'narcissism' in this atmosphere that surrounded my mother, but, as Freud suggests, this might be construed as a 'triumph' in light of 'the unkindness of the real circumstances' – Andrew's epilepsy but also some shadow from my dear mother's earlier life.

We were all on her journey together, my mother in the driver's seat, a position she enjoyed so much more than my father did. My mother drove fast, my father slowly. Driving with my father could feel very precarious, with a lot of stopping and starting and straying onto the wrong side of the road. There were many near misses, whichever parent was driving, and these near misses were all a part of the humour of our situation. Suddenly my mother would skid to a halt by the side of the road and whip out a picnic before you could say 'Abracadabra!' More informal eating arrangements have been my mother's forte – meals she continues to produce (well into her eighties now) as if by sleight of hand.

As a child I believed my mother could make a picnic work anywhere in the world or even in amongst the craters on the moon – she could conjure a meal in the paradise of a wildflower meadow in Somerset or on the smallest piece of grass beside a motorway, the traffic roaring by. The coming together for a meal was what counted. There was something humorous about the proceedings in that I could feel very uncomfortable physically on that piece of grass beside the noisy road, whilst still immensely enjoying the tumble of sandwiches and oranges and chocolate bars my mother seemed to juggle.

Cezanne's paintings remind me of my mother and her very deep love of the countryside in Dorset and Somerset – her passion for flowers, the fruits of the land and the ordinary life of farmers. Last week she wrapped some fresh green beans in newspaper for me to take home after a visit. She no longer has a garden but continues to seek out fresh produce up and down the Surrey lanes. Only recently she discovered some allotments on high open ground. My mother is not planning to take one herself now she is in her eighties, but she loves to look at the spread of produce rooted in these little patches of ground. My mother's sympathies have always lain with the workers of the land and of the world. Her instincts are egalitarian, even when she sounds a little haughty and aristocratic. She left her rich aristocratic family behind (along with any chance of an inheritance) at the age of seventeen and only occasionally looked back at that cruelty she has never revealed. Her marriage to a half Russian, metropolitan psychiatrist, who had grown up in Bloomsbury, sealed the rejection of her 'county' roots.

I think of my mother when contemplating Cezanne's *Still Life with Water Jug* (c 1892-93), another key work owned by Frank Stoop. I came upon the picture at the National Gallery a few years ago and have appreciated the picture without looking into the details of the holding. In my thinking about Frank, the Stoop bequest becomes a democratic and open-handed gesture to the world. Even though he had hoped the bequest would remain in one gallery after his death, he does not mind 'overmuch'.[78] Here are my pictures, he says – look and enjoy, come share my pleasure! Anyone is welcome at his picnic of paintings so long as they are prepared to tuck in with good humour and not be too precious about art. Let the pictures breathe.

I first saw Cezanne's *Still Life with Water Jug* at the National Gallery in the summer of 2006, the same year as I came upon John Frederick Lewis's *The Courtyard* at the old Tate and Cezanne's *The Gardener Vallier* at the Cezanne in Britain exhibition. I can be precise about the date as I wrote, but never sent, a postcard of the picture to Betty and Laurie (Bradbury):

> *Hoping all is well with you and that you're not overwhelmed by this heat! I'm rather sweltering in my 'garret'. I came upon this painting by Cezanne – so beautiful. The summer is going too fast. Hoping to speak soon. with lots of love, Gillxxx*

I cannot remember why I did not send the card, but in moving to my studio, I came upon the postcard of the picture in among the papers

---

[78] This word is often used by Thomas Hardy (a West country poet who reminds me of my mother) in his poems.

in my old seafarer's chest. Only yesterday I saw the painting with my students and was lifted up, as always, when coming upon the lightness Cezanne achieved in this work. In this picture he 'travels light' in my mother's sense. This might have been a meal set out by her and, whenever I see the painting, it makes me smile.

Still Life with Water Jug is a picture of an ordinary table that might be used for anything – for eating at or working or simply as a space that might be filled, half-filled or left fallow. The table top (all we see) is parallel to the picture plane and at a slight sideways tilt, but the al fresco picnic does not appear to be in danger of falling to the floor. The table and its contents fill the bottom half of the painting and a nicely bellied teal jug is the only object standing at the back of the surface. Almost at the centre there's a plain plate of six or seven apples. The plate's edge touches the bottom of the jug and next to it there is some bread roughly sliced in two pieces. The plate, jug and bread might be held in the semi-circle I found myself tracing (yesterday) with my forefinger when talking with the students about this picture.

There are six or seven more apples scattered about the table, along with crumpled white napkins and a dishevelled cloth that covers just half of the table. You might imagine the cloth suddenly being pulled away from beneath this impromptu arrangement by a magician – Hey presto! The feast remains on the table, only tilting a little after the trick the artist-magician has played. In the 'unfinished' dirty white background I see a sleeve and even the hint of a man's body – Cezanne himself perhaps contemplating a hastily eaten meal. Around the teal jug there is moss-green paint, as though the water or the wine were cooling. Apart from the jug this still life is barely still. The completeness of the painting lies in its makeshift, mobile quality.

When I was eight years old a psychiatrist colleague of my father's, Peter Mellett, who visited every so often and was passionate about art and poetry (a discovery I made long after those visits), turned to me one lunchtime and exclaimed, 'Look, Gill – look at the table! Everything is scattered about and see, what lovely colours and the apples look delicious! What an appetising picnic or I should say what a splendid picture Mum made for us to eat and to look at!'

Peter chuckled with good humour at this visual joke and I'm eight years old again entranced by the strangest things he says when he comes to dinner, asking me to look in all directions at the things he noticed. I'm nervous I'll get the answer wrong, but that doesn't seem to be the point. Peter wants me to enjoy and relish what I see, the 'splendid picture' my mother had made. I could applaud my mother's humour and spirit as she conjured meals out of thin air, but the idea of seeing the meal as a 'picture' was beyond me. At some level, though, I felt sure that I was yet to find a key to this puzzle. Like Lewis Carroll's Alice at the beginning of her story I could only catch glimpses of the pictures in the art garden.

I would feel bereft when my mother disappeared (along with her magic) to run the house and look after Andrew, her ears and eyes forever on the alert should he fall or lose consciousness. I wished I could see what my father's friend, Peter, saw. To enjoy anything independently with a child's natural spontaneity, was a betrayal in the face of my brother's epilepsy. To develop my own life and humour would mean being outside the magic circle of my mother, father and myself, with Andrew in our midst and at the centre of our anxious but loving gaze. My much younger siblings, Robert and Liz, were part of what felt like a second, more ordinary family I would often envy bitterly.

I persisted, though, in imagining a future where I might be more at liberty. I think I can. I think I can, like 'the little train that could' in the story-book my mother read to me over and over again in the course of my childhood at my request, with both of us laughing at the little train's triumph in conclusion. [79] One day perhaps I would understand what Peter was saying and why the effort made by the little train in the book has always felt so humorous but nigh impossible.

In my sixties I arrive at a point where I can appreciate not knowing too much may be the key to living well. I no longer believe that the

---

[79] See p. 16 for details of the 'little train'

adults have all the answers and that my mother's magic will solve everything. I am beginning to look around and about without getting giddy like my brother in a seizure or me spinning in his shadow. My childlessness can at times weigh less heavily on my spirit. I can be reassured that one can be free from what I have perceived as the terrible burden of caring for a very ill child. I am beginning to let go of the guilt and shame I have felt (in memory of my brother) in allowing myself to experience ordinary feelings of joy. I am beginning to 'travel light' in the way my mother suggested.

Life is the greatest art form of all and now I can take whatever road (that looks promising) I choose, following the signs more intuitively and naturally than I have been able to do up until now.

Yes. Now I can see a way. Everything around me grows still. There isn't even the slightest breeze. I am in my studio in real time. The studio floor is at a slight tilt in places because it was built in the seventeenth century and this cornerstone of the almshouse block has seen all kinds of people to-ing and fro-ing down the centuries – church men and women, poor scholars and a host of others. Only last week a colleague, an art historian, told me (as if we were sharing a good joke) that he had lived near my studio once upon a time and had visited the gallery and the park with much pleasure. I realise that I have taken up residence in a very small and a reassuringly old world. This place was once a hub of church politics and prayer. Now people take photos of wedding parties emerging into the courtyard from the chapel. I often feel I've stepped into one of Anthony Trollope's novels, *The Warden* for instance, but the wedding parties and the cameras clicking all around remind me this is the twenty-first century – a century in which I and other like-minded friends (now we are on the cusp of getting old) can often find ourselves at odds.

Those of us few will joyfully, mournfully, painfully and with good humour, I feel sure – we will stay true to the spirit of the place.

I am back in the Surrey garden at *Holmwood* in my early childhood. The early summer sun is high in the sky and our six cats (one tabby, three black, two tortoise-shell) are lounging on the steps – like a family come to rest for a while between the upper and lower lawns. My elder brother, Andrew, and I, have gathered and are spilling over with a harvest of apples we carry in two of our mother's wicker baskets. We set them down on the large rectangular lawn and join our parents, who are seated at the small folding garden table. My two small siblings are running over from the swing beneath the cherry tree, where they were taking turns to push one another up and down beneath a storm of late blossom. Everyone is laughing in this picture.

My mother's lunch is simple – bread and cheese and apples, jugs of water and wine to wash them down, Cezanne-style. The six cats continue to enjoy the sun. On cold winter nights one or two cats will curl up on the boiler in the kitchen.

I first saw a much earlier painting by Cezanne, *The Stove in the Studio* (not one of Frank's), in 2002 at the National Gallery. I came upon the picture after one of my visits with students. My mind is often in a state of over-excitement when looking at paintings with a class. The students' enthusiasm is exhilarating and I range about with them in spirit, if not in my body that begins to grow tired, or in my mind that craves more solitude these days. It is a pleasure to be with my students, but there is relief when my charges have dispersed and I can slow down, focus.

My first response to *The Stove* was one of relief, despite the bleakness of the setting. I enjoyed being alone with the picture. This small painting is defined by blackness and dark grey – black walls and an ancient grey boiler upon which there is a cauldron. Despite the glimpse of a flame inside the boiler, there is nothing identifiable being cooked. Beneath the stove there is a pile of silver grey ashes and behind it there is the light brown back of a large canvas, its face turned to the wall. This provides a promising focus in the overriding darkness. Cezanne's palette, along with a small brightly coloured painting and a blob of white on the walls, appear to float in the shade.

I love this painting for its unromantic sentiment. This might be anyone's studio in 1860s Paris when Cezanne was beginning to make a name for himself. The blackness is, for me, an idea of a black canvas as opposed to the more familiar tabula rasa, the blank space, the white sheet upon which countless writers and artists have imagined and inscribed themselves. Cezanne's is a darkness from which something beautiful may emerge – less a phoenix arising from the silver grey ashes than an idea that is about to be slowly warmed into life once the stove is lit.

The austerity of Cezanne's vocation is, in *The Stove*, there for all to see. He believed in his work, even if he felt crowded by the metropolitan song and dance, the over-weaning city ambitions he witnessed all around him in Paris. In Cezanne's friend, Emile Zola's novel, *L'Oeuvre*, there is a description of an artist's studio (based on Cezanne's) in which there is a canvas turned to face the wall, as in Cezanne's painting.

> *It was the large canvas at which the painter was working, and which he pushed against the wall every night, the better to judge it on the morrow in the surprise of the first glance.*[80]

In my reading of the painting, the back of the large canvas will, in good time, be turned around to reveal itself and this may come as a surprise, both to the artist himself and to the viewer – the flourishing green upon green and the earth colours, the tones Cezanne worked with throughout his career, will be seen in all their glory, along with the apples that have yet to show themselves in the fullness of their fruit. I hope my mother might appreciate the art in all the stoves she has warmed and meals and journeys she has made for her family. We shall all raise a glass to her in celebration of her immense achievement in keeping the show on the road and us in good humour.

When my father was in his final years at the Surrey nursing home, looking out of his large window in the L shaped room on the ground floor of the comfortable villa, I would sometimes take a picnic,

---

[80] Emile Zola, *L'Oeuvre*, 1886

especially in summer.   On my thirty-sixth birthday I brought, in a
wicker basket, smoked salmon, cream cheese, water biscuits and
apples, accompanied by a bottle of chilled Vouvray – the wine I had
chosen for its freshness and light.   My father didn't eat or drink much
at this time but I could see he enjoyed the idea of a picnic. I believe
he was remembering my mother and her al fresco feasts.   I dressed
the small coffee table with a red checked tablecloth and fed my father,
his knees tucked neatly beneath the hospital table, from the picnic on
the lower table.

I had recreated the scene of the card table that had been a fixture
in his sitting-room in his later years in the mid to late eighties. There
he ate all his meals, mostly alone (my parents had divorced a decade
before) except for breakfast which he took in the large kitchen. The
green snooker baize, that covered the card table back then, grew
dull with use, but recently I have had it restored by Karen at the Chair
Sanctuary, a workshop to the east of my studio – the table has come
into its own again over twenty years after my father's death. The green
baize is a strong, vibrant colour rather like Cezanne's ubiquitous green.

After my parents separated in the late 1970s I returned to my father
and became his companion for a while. We shared many a meal and,
like Estragon and Vladimir in Samuel Beckett's *Waiting for Godot*, [81]
we spent what seemed a life-time together (although it was only a few
years), as if waiting for someone to arrive and resolve our dilemma.
No-one ever did of course. We had a very strong affinity that kept us
close. We were both very afraid of the world and shunned, resisted,
taking to that jostling Shakespearian stage of many players, along with
all those wearying exits and entrances. 'I don't go to the theatre much,'
Samuel Beckett said with a wry smile to a journalist in a Dublin pub,
who had asked him about the state of contemporary theatre.

Today I appreciate the sense of belonging my father carried about
with him, even though a deepening melancholy and depression were
habitual.   His two cats (a grey mother and her delicate black daughter)

---

[81] **Samuel Beckett,** *Waiting for Godot,* **1953/1955**

came after the six cats of my childhood and they sat on the boiler in his kitchen, warming themselves. There he is, playing chess at the faded card table, the cats brushing up against his legs and sometimes jumping up onto the table, at which my father gently shoos them away. His head is bent over the board like Rodin's thinker (*Le Penseur,* 1904). A Beckettian, a dark humorist, without knowing it (he is too deep in melancholy) he does not move for long periods and then slowly picks up the knight (the most romantic and elusive piece on the board) to place it one square up and two sideways. Is he recollecting his analysis with Paula Heimann and feeling that he had not come up to scratch? Or has he forgiven himself for his failings? Has he recognised hers? Analysts are fallible after all.

I think he might be recalling my young mother when they met and fell in love in central London in the late 1940s. He remembers her preparing sumptuous meals for a growing family. He looks up from the dull green baize, wishing she were here. My parents both had an appreciation of life's humour, albeit they possessed different styles of making us laugh. Freud concludes his essay on humour, suggesting that the super-ego speaks in humour 'kindly words of comfort to the intimidated ego' – an ego overwhelmed with difficulty and trauma.

> *[...] if the super-ego tries, by means of humour, to console the ego and protect it from suffering, this does not contradict its origin in parental agency.*[82]

I love Freud's idea of a kindly, parental super-ego. In my learning these psychoanalytic terms at my father's knee, the super-ego (first of all I thought it was a giant egg!) seemed very ominous and overbearing, a fearful form of authority. In retrospect I think, as Andrew grew taller and larger than the rest of the family, and as his psychosis developed and grew in his late teens, my brother became my idea of a fearful super-ego. He towered over the family, his anger and pain assuming an authority we all feared. We lost sight of the small boy who had suffered so unbearably and for so long.

---

[82] Ibid, 166

7

Red Stone Dancer

'the girl who steps along' [83]

H enri Gaudier-Brzeska was one of the 'youthful spirits'[84] ushered into the Tate by Frank Stoop. Gaudier's short sharp life and work (he was killed in 1915, aged thirty-four, fighting in the trenches during the First World War) were full of dynamism and quickness and concentrations of heightened emotion. One of his most well known works, *Red Stone Dancer* (c 1913), is a sculpture in red Mansfield stone, which Frank gifted to the Tate through the Contemporary Art Society in 1930 and listed in the *Stoop Bequest* (Appendix 1). This squat sculpture, measuring a foot and a half tall by nine inches wide, has for many years drawn my eye at the Tate and the recent knowledge that the work was owned by Frank Stoop invests it with a fresh surge of interest. It is a figure charged with energy and contorted by some powerful emotion. I have thought of the figure as male but it is in fact female. She seems to be struggling to free herself from something, her arms caught up

---

[83] Freud, 'Delusions and Dreams in Jensen's *Gradiva*', 11, IX (1906 – 1908) ibid
[84] See p. 92

around her head, as though she were attempting to rid her mind of its thoughts. Her knees bend as if she would like to leap out of the stone that petrifies her movement.

Freud's long essay, 'Delusions & Dreams in Jensen's *Gradiva*' comes to mind. The essay, Freud's first psychoanalytic study of a work of literature, was published in 1907 and refers to the novella by the German writer, Wilhelm Jensen, *Gradiva: Ein Pompejanisches Phantasiestuck* (1903).

> *A young archaeologist, Norbert Hanold, had discovered in a museum of antiquities in Rome a relief [real] which had so immensely attracted him that he was greatly pleased at obtaining an excellent plaster cast of it which he could hang in his study in a German university town and gaze at with interest. The sculpture represented a fully-grown girl stepping along, with her flowing dress a little pulled up so as to reveal her sandalled feet. One foot rested squarely on the ground; the other, lifted from the ground in the act of following after, touched it only with the tips of the toes, while the sole and heel rose almost perpendicularly.*
>
> *[...] Norbert's imagination was occupied with the sculpture without ceasing. He found something 'of to-day' about it, as though the artist had had a glimpse in the street and captured it 'from the life'. He gave the girl thus pictured as she stepped along the name of 'Gradiva' - 'the girl who steps along'.*[85]

Norbert finds it 'hard to fit her quiet, calm nature into the busy life of a capital city.' He convinces himself that 'she must be transported to Pompeii'[86] and travels to the ancient settlement, where he meets a woman who seems to be Gradiva, but is in fact (he realises) Zoe, a childhood sweetheart, whose name, he tells her, 'means life'[87].

---

[85] Ibid, 10 – 11

[86] Ibid, 11

[87] Ibid, 21

Freud analyses this meeting as evidence of the repression of his erotic desire for Zoe now come to light.

> In his [Jensen's] last simile [...] of the 'childhood friend who has been dug out of the ruins' – the author has presented us with the key to the symbolism of which the hero's delusion made use in disguising his repressed memory. There is, in fact, no better analogy for repression, by which something in the mind is at once made inaccessible and preserved, than burial of the sort to which Pompeii fell a victim and from which it could emerge once more through the work of spades.[88]

Zoe/Gradiva does, though, in Jensen's story have the last word:

> They had arrived again at the Hercules gate where, at the beginning of the Strada Consolare, old stepping stones crossed the street. Norbert Hanold stopped before them and said with a peculiar tone, 'Please go ahead here.' A merry, comprehending, laughing expression lurked around his companion's mouth, and, raising her dress slightly with her left hand, Gradiva rediviva Zoe Bertgang, viewed by him with dreamily observing eyes, crossed with her calmly buoyant walk, through the sunlight, over the stepping-stones, to the other side of the street.[89]

Freud is primarily concerned with bringing the repressed erotic content of Jensen's/Norbert's phantasy to light and this is fascinating in itself. Today, though, in making a connection between Gaudier's *Red Stone Dancer* and Freud's Gradiva, I am struck primarily by Gradiva/Zoe's moving in and out of phantasy and reality, 'through' the sunlight and 'over' the stepping-stones. She has been found by her childhood admirer and become a living form in his eyes but, as an aesthetic figure of the early twentieth century, she still has a way to go if she is to find

---

[88] Ibid, 40

[89] Wilhelm Jensen, *Gradiva: Ein Pompejanisches Phantasiestuck*, 1903

the living woman in herself. Her lover's eyes are 'dreamily observing' her like the flaneur of the period, who at that time was still struggling to 'see' and comprehend the 'new woman' stepping out and emerging in the modern city.

It is interesting that Jensen had to relocate Gradiva from the modern city life of Rome to Pompeii, a more romantic and archaeological destination. The stepping-stones Gradiva/Zoe walks over in conclusion might still be in a phantasy realm below or above ground.

Gaudier's *Red Stone Dancer*, which appeared just ten years after Jensen's *Gradiva*, presents a very different figure but I connect the two pieces in my mind. I like the idea of Gradiva/Zoe's movement and of her crossing over. She escapes her lover's desire to aestheticise and make her more permanent in his imagination. She is defined in and by her movements in her old lover's mind and by her own volition in the world outside his imagination, although they are, of course, both the products of Jensen's mind and then of Freud's. She is graceful and elusive and strong in my mind, and I hope she finds a place for herself and then maybe, if the conditions are right, for her lover.

Last year I talked with my therapist about *Red Stone Dancer*. He seemed particularly interested when I demonstrated (laying there on his firm but comfortable couch) with my arms and hands, how the figure's arms are caught up around her head in a state of heightened, even appalling tension. Her body twists and bends in some life and death struggle for liberty. These are my writer's words. When I lay there on the couch I expressed myself much less fluently, as though I preferred him to *see* how my body was registering my response to Gaudier's sculpture. A year later I have returned to the same subject and, as I write, I am anticipating my next therapeutic session tomorrow afternoon.

In the meantime I turn to a writer who has much to say about *Red Stone Dancer*.

> *Red Stone Dancer* shows a figure in powerful motion. Elaborating on Rodin's idea of movement captured at the moment of transition from one pose to another, Gaudier introduces here the Vorticist postulate of a figure portrayed

at its point of most compressed energy, as if she is about to metaphorically burst into a dance.

The splayed feet and taut legs give a powerful impression of movement checked. This is also emphasised in the positioning of the upraised arms. [...] The face, sensitively observed in the earlier **Dancer,** *has been replaced by a triangle.*

[...] Red Stone Dancer is stocky and unashamedly pugnacious in impact, with a triangle imposed on her otherwise featureless face and equally geometric forms of her breasts. The entire body defies anatomical convention by twisting and bending in unlikely directions.[90]

In Jensen's novella Norbert gives the ancient relief the name, Gradiva, 'which he constructed on the model of an epithet of the war-god striding into battle – 'Mars Gradivus'.'[91] With the help of Richard Cork's words I find the connection between Gradiva/Zoe and Gaudier's *Red Stone Dancer*. The figures are both 'captured at the moment of transition from one pose to another' (Cork) but only Gaudier (what a difference ten years can make and also the impending First World War in which Gaudier would be killed) takes the Vorticist step forward in locating distorted and repressed emotions in a female body that is beautifully ugly in her thwarted expression.

Gradiva has one foot on the ground and the other 'lifted from the ground in the act of following after'[92] at the beginning of Freud's account and in Jensen's conclusion she is moving over the stepping-stones on her way to the other side of the street. In 1913 the Futurist, Stanley Cursiter's wonderful painting, *The Sensation of Crossing the Street*, appeared and was later used by Penguin Classics on the front cover of Virginia Woolf's *Mrs Dalloway* (1925) in 2000. Gradiva/Zoe then, in our readers' eyes, became a contemporary woman crossing

---

[90] Richard Cork, *Grove Art Online*, c 2009

[91] Ibid, 50

[92] Ibid, 10

the street in the twenty-first century and in my classroom when I teach *Mrs Dalloway*.

I am identified with Gaudier's *Red Stone Dancer* in that I have felt in my life very much in the grip of powerful emotions of love, hate, envy, joy, anger... and it has taken a lot of psychoanalytic therapy to help me express these emotions and also understand and come to terms with the roots of the uglier feelings, which have arrested the potential to experience love more fully. It has taken me this long to realise that growing up in the presence of my brother's seizures was like being perpetually turned to stone as I waited for them (and also me by association) to end. They literally struck me dumb and I began to pride myself on being still as a statue, even admired the aesthetic I unconsciously honed as I grew.

I loved and was very good at dancing – in the sixties I embraced the twist, the shake, the cool routines of Tamla Motown – but I was on auto, a dancing machine I could start up and stop at will.

I have wanted, though, to be like the graceful, charming Gradiva – to be light on my feet as I barely touch ground and to exist just beyond any human grasp on my affections. To escape has been my greatest of pleasures – to escape the monotony and relentless power of Andrew's seizures that replicated death in every hour of our days together. I loved my brother deeply and felt scarcely bearable compassion for his suffering. Guilt at wishing the seizures away and even wanting to put my brother out of his terrible pain and misery in his later years, has also turned me to stone, but now I am finding ways to countenance this difficult past and to move on, put my best foot forward and make that crossing without knowing where I'll land exactly.

Gaudier's dancer reminds me of that modern Victorian, Robert Browning's bracing and clever poem, 'Fra Lippo Lippi' (*Men & Women*, 1855), which recounts the story of the real Renaissance painter and friar, for whom life was gloriously carnal in spite of his spiritual vocation. In the poem he paints 'saints and saints and saints again' on the walls of his church, whilst gasping for the fresh air of the streets. Lippi escapes the Florentine monastery by night to carouse and chase women, celebrating 'the value and significance of flesh'. I studied this poem at A Level and have loved its playful sensuality ever since, even though there have been long years when my books gathered dust or were jettisoned along the many pathways I took. I did, though, hold onto my Robert Browning volume. A couple of lines have become a mantra for me in more recent years, buoying up my spirits:

> This world's no blot for us,
> Nor blank; it means intensely, and means good:
> To find its meaning is my meat and drink.

Browning struggled to find a form of poetry that would give voice to an individual's energies and emotions and to a mind that is in perpetual motion – the 'mind in difficulties' Walter Bagehot describes in his 1864 essay on Tennyson and Browning. [93] Gaudier is a kindred spirit coming after Browning's bold experiments.

I find myself returning to another book that has travelled with me, defying my negations, since I was studying for my A Levels back in the late sixties. There are a multitude of books I have jettisoned over the years. This little book, though, *English Critical Essays on 19th century poetry,* edited by Edmund D. Jones and published by Oxford University Press, I have held onto along with Browning and Tennyson, George Eliot and Thomas Hardy. My writing in the margins is very child-like and I notice, in leafing through the essays now, how many times I write the word 'simplicity' as though that idea was important to my adolescent mind. Or was that my English teacher's emphasis? I wonder. The idea of simplicity means a great deal to me now – it means 'intensely, and means good'. To find its meaning is my meat and drink.

In the middle of writing this chapter I have been very pleasantly interrupted by a Sainsbury's delivery of food and wine. The bags were handed to me by Mitch Jacob, who is an artist when not delivering other people's 'meat and drink'. This is the second time he has come with my Sainsbury's order and we picked up where we left off (about a month

---

[93] Edmund D. Jones (Ed), *English Critical Essays on 19th century poetry,* 1916/1968

ago) in our talk about art. Mitch took part in a collaborative project and exhibition, *Drawing from Turner* (2006-2007) at Tate Britain. The word 'copy' was avoided so that the artists could work with the paintings closely in order to produce their own work. Mitch worked with J.M.W. Turner's *The Brocklesbury Mausoleum Seen Among Trees*, 1798, and in the drawing that resulted, the trees look younger than in Turner's work. Mitch Jacob has given the mausoleum new life in the twenty-first century. I am impressed by the transparent love of art that sustains him whilst working for a supermarket chain. Needs must, he smiles.

I return to my writing which has been invigorated by this fresh and unexpected conversation. I hope Mitch arrives on my doorstep again. I wonder if he is Jewish. My therapist's Italian name has been a source of fascination ever since I began to see him a year or so ago. I have romanticised his origins, which are actually in Manchester. He is amused by my wondering and I think he sometimes smiles at my jokes in his armchair at the foot of the couch. His suggestions are invariably imperceptible and subtle like a benign snake winding its way into my thoughts. I think of myself as a Fra Lippo Lippi carousing in the Peckham streets, dropping by to see 'my Italian'.

I pause on his couch to take breath. For liberty I gasp.

Liberty is a word I am growing to savour, in spite of my fear that freedom (at least the limited freedoms some of us are lucky enough to enjoy) is forever beyond my grasp. I like the simplicity of the word and my therapist's quiet acceptance of my own very wordy processes. He seeks to divert me into less verbal trains of feeling and onto less language-strewn paths. I often cannot stop talking in his presence and yet I struggle to free myself from words. This is a dilemma, a paradox.

I am the red stone dancer and I love Frank Stoop, that familiar stranger in my imagination, for collecting this piece. I am hopeful that the dancer will find a freer form. I am Gradiva/Zoe picking her way across the street to who knows where.

Gaudier made *Red Stone Dancer* circa 1913, on the cusp of the First World War, in which he would fight with tenacious energy before being killed in the trenches at Neuville-St.-Vaast in 1915. During his time in the French army he sculpted a figure out of the butt of a rifle taken from a German soldier to express a gentler order of feeling. My brother, Andrew, foreseeing an early death as the epilepsy worsened, made himself a perfectly symmetrical coffin and a large stage on which to play the guitar in the upturned coffin. Andrew made things out of wood and in his latter years believed he was Jesus, the carpenter. My brother was a genius but I feared his rage against the world that grew along with his illness. Robert Browning wrote about hatred and spite in his poetry and I have found Andrew's but also my own reflection.

In her autobiography, Enid Bagnold (who was sculpted by Gaudier) paid tribute to the artist's brilliance whilst acknowledging that she found him difficult to like personally. She refers to the artist, Claud Lovat Fraser, being excited by Gaudier's talent but put off by the artist himself:

> *Lovat, most indulgent of men, would never express dislike, but he would not waste time on Gaudier's burning, voluble, cascading talk, though he deeply respected his art. I didn't like him either; and Gaudier on his side found us both middleclass. We had no idea then of his crippling poverty. He had no time for talk because he was out of work. Too proud to say so he talked instead of eating. He didn't want to know what people were like. He rushed at them, held them, poured his thoughts over them, and when in response, they said ten words his impatience overflowed; he jabbed and wounded and the blood flowed.*[94]

I warm to the idea of Gaudier's 'cascading talk' whilst being repelled by its insistence. He seems to have talked and worked as if he were on the battlefield. A Vorticist, he applauded the machine age and its capacity for violence. And yet he desired a gentler order of feeling. My brother did not talk incessantly. His anger and rage did not need to be spoken. They filled his large frame for all to see. William Blake's words from *The Tyger* (1798) ring true: 'What immortal hand or eye/ Dare frame thy fearful symmetry?'

---

[94] Enid Bagnold, *Enid Bagnold's Autobiography*, 1969

I was the one who, after a long period of relative silence, found that I could not stop talking. There was so much to talk about. I have at times 'jabbed' at and 'wounded' my friends and my family. I am sorry for that aggression but sometimes I simply must be heard. My therapist listens patiently. I often wonder how on earth he can be so quiet in his listening to me. Sometimes the fifty minutes feel good and long as I've made the most of the time, articulating myself clearly and making fruitful connections. Then I talk more slowly and allow myself to pause. I engage in conversation with my therapist or he engages me. At other times the words seem to block the way to more helpful 'meaning' and then I leave with a feeling that I've not allowed myself the real time that defines my presence on the couch. Words can so often mask despair and pain and appetite. Pauses and comfortable silences can bear fruit.

What more is there of interest to me in Gaudier's short, sharp and very sad story?

The artist was born in 1891 in St. Jean de Brayer, a small village near Orleans, his father a carpenter. He received no formal art training but won scholarships to Bristol in 1907 and Nuremberg in 1909, moving to Paris in 1910, where he would establish a career as an artist. In 1910 he moved to London with Sophie Brzeska, a Polish writer he had met in Paris. He was nineteen years old and at thirty-seven she was twice his age. Henri annexed her surname to his and they never married. The younger man and older woman both struggled with poverty and acute anxiety, inevitably leading to mental health problems. Their relationship was, according to H.S. Ede (who acquired Sophie's estate in 1927), mostly non-sexual, with Sophie buying Gaudier prostitutes every so often. In London they pretended to be siblings. Sadly Sophie would die in a Gloucestershire psychiatric hospital at Barwood in 1925. She was in her early fifties.[95]

I am struck by the couple's sibling pretence. I had a close and intense relationship with Andrew. I have written about his illness and

---

[95] H.S. Ede, *Savage Messiah*, 1931. The film adaptation, *Savage Messiah*, directed by Ken Russell, was released in 1972.

later psychosis in *The Sound of Turquoise*, in which I describe us as 'twin souls' living in the awful knowledge of epilepsy and its predations that interrupted our life together.

Madeline Clements, in her review in *The Times Literary Supplement* (19.3.2010) writes:

> *Gill Gregory's* The Sound of Turquoise *breathes life into the experiences of her White Russian grandfather [...] and also puzzles over the pieces of her elder brother Andrew's life, repeatedly shattered by epileptic fits.*
>
> *This is a story told in third person and 'based on real histories', designed to map the 'invisible pathways' its child-narrator, Meg – who is Gregory herself – 'keeps on bearing in mind'. Gregory retires from the scene of her gentle, lyrical life history, creating a space in which her alter ego, 'Meg', who grows up in 1960s Surrey and London, can relive and review her experiences.*
>
> *Ever preoccupied with the illness of Andrew, we watch Meg as she haunts the periphery, keeping a crucial eye for the tell-tale signs of a violent fit or 'grand mal', that will dictate their exile from [belonging in the worlds of other teenagers]. Meg's crippling childhood concern with her brother's epilepsy, and her gnawing adult guilt at having wanted to run from him, bring drama to Gregory's quietly emotional reimagining of the harsh reality.*

The idea of my book's gentle lyricism continues to surprise me. I had felt at the time of writing *The Sound of Turquoise* that it was a rather noisy, demanding book. Reading Clements's review helped me to see my book and myself with more clarity. I can now see the figures of both Gradiva/Zoe and of Gaudier's dancer in my earlier book. Gradiva tells her story gracefully and lyrically whilst Gaudier's dancer struggles to express the ugliness of her pain and anger. I had wanted to spare my readers any messy outbursts and now I am finding in this book, *The Studio*, that articulating myself in much greater detail and non-fictionally has and is creating many pathways for my pain. I do not care to shout my story, preferring the civilities of prose that unfold themselves in due course.

I am taking my cue from Jensen and Freud's Gradiva/Zoe in finding my way into and then out of pictures or sculptures: I put my best foot forwards, treading carefully over the stepping stones that will take me (I hope) to the other side of trauma and its wearily destructive repetitions.

In the presence of my therapist, I am experiencing moments of pure joy. I sometimes feel like dancing down his stairs before disappearing into the night that is or at least seems balmy and 'southern' for a while after a good session. Like Browning's Fra Lippo Lippi I am out on a night's carouse, dropping by at *Cafe Viva* in Choumert Road where people are gathering for an opening of works by a local artist.

The surrogate sibling relationship, the coupling of Gaudier and Brzeska , reminds me of myself and Andrew, locked (like the Red Stone Dancer) in a petrified embrace that held me in its grip long after Andrew's death in 1977.

> I love thee with the passion put to use
> In my old griefs, and with my childhood's faith.
> I love thee with a love I seemed to lose
> With my lost saints, I love thee with the breath,
> Smiles, tears, of all my life! – and, if God choose,
> I shall but love thee better after death.[96]

At the age of thirty-four Elizabeth Barrett Browning (Robert Browning was her younger husband by six years) lost her elder brother, Edward, when he drowned off the Devonshire coast in 1840. In recollecting her impassioned sonnet (a little monument to grief) Andrew becomes my 'lost saint'.

I sense affection in my therapist's eyes when he greets me and says goodbye at the beginning and the end of the session. I struggle in his

---

[96] Elizabeth Barrett Browning, Sonnet XLIII, 'Sonnets from the Portuguese' (1850), *Selected Poems*, Ed. Margaret Forster, 1992

presence to overcome guilt and to bear with the pain of compassion. On the mortuary slab after he died, Andrew lay with his mouth wide open, rigid in rigor mortis. The nurses had been unable to close his mouth after the oxygen was turned off and he was 'freed' (the horrible irony) from the apparatus. Draped in a purple pall, with a gold cross emblazoned on the cloth, he looked like a 'savage messiah' (the term used to describe Gaudier) in his suffering. I close Andrew's wide-open mouth and its silent scream.

On my desk there sits a squat stone incubus. Like Gaudier's dancer she is scrunched into herself, her troll-like mouth open with her left hand held inside the cavity, as if about to vomit up any sustenance I might offer, daring me to take her in hand. Her ears have broken off with age or was it rage? Where is this little figure from? No-one in my family can remember who owned this heirloom. My grandparents mixed in artistic bohemian circles. My grandfather, Alexis, was an art collector, although his taste was for the English landscapes of John Constable and Thomas Gainsborough. Maybe, though, Gaudier himself made my little scrunched figure? Alexis might have met him at a soiree. Who knows? Did someone use her as a paperweight? Her back is slightly hunched, as if the years spent containing her anger had fixed her for eternity in this stance. Her feet are turned inwards, one resting on the other. She gives the impression of being totally sealed off and yet the open mouth suggests she may have something more to say.

Suddenly the incubus grows sweet in her fury. I do not need to hide her in a corner. She can take her place on my desk or anywhere she chooses. She is a little devil I can live with and even enjoy.

SOURCES

Richard Cork, 'Henri Gaudier-Brzeska', *Kettle's Yard Collection,* 2009
Tate Britain website

8

Animals Gather in Dulwich Park

I dreamt that it was night and that I was lying in my bed. (My bed stood with its foot towards the window; in front of the window there was a row of old walnut trees [...]) [97]

I count all the animals and birds in the fourteen sketches by Henri Gaudier-Brzeska on Frank Stoop's list of bequests. There are nine animals, six birds and four vultures. Some of the animals are in pairs and others are alone. A modern day ark would not insist on pairs. I imagine the birds (who have followed the ark to its destination) alighting on the branches of the trees in a green wooded terrain. The four vultures hover. The animals I see in my mind's eye stretch their legs after such a long journey and look around them at this very English park at my door. The ark has arrived at the Lodge inside the gates that are in view from my studio.

If the animals and birds prefer to range further afield, there is the American garden with its famous dells of rhododendrons on the far eastern side of the park, which Queen Mary of Teck (the consort of George V) visited in a carriage every spring. On this more secluded side of the park I came upon (this spring) a small family party enjoying

---

[97] Freud, 'From the History of an Infantile Neurosis', 29, XVII (1917 – 1919) ibid

a picnic in one of the dells. In seeing them they struck me as a group that came truly alive in this quiet spot. Similarly Gaudier-Brzeska's pen and ink drawings become 'living forms' [98] beside the Lodge in my view as I write about them.

Gaudier had arrived in London with his surrogate sibling, Sophie, in 1911 and the drawings were sketched circa 1912 – 1913:

> The artist Claude Lovat Fraser supported Gaudier in several ways, including the gift of tickets to Regents Park Zoo in London. There Gaudier spent his weekends sketching the animals so quickly that the ink was often still wet as he turned the page. With a few elegant lines and no shading, he managed to convey three-dimensional form and capture a momentary view of a beast in movement. [99]

The sketches are like drawings in a child's storybook. Most of Gaudier's animals and birds do not look very wild. His animals reveal another side to the Vorticist and 'savage messiah'. There he was, child-like, at Regent's Park Zoo (the antithesis of a wilderness) sketching the animals as he saw them.

Like Gaudier, I viewed them one by one as they were laid out before me by Marilyne Auriat, a registrar at the Prints & Drawings Room at Tate Britain. I have often resisted too much 'method', let alone 'methodology', a word that paralyses my imagination, but there does of course need to be some order, and standing the animals in a line is as good a way as any. Marilyne took me into one of the study rooms and laid out Gaudier's drawings on writing slopes so that I could study them closely. I felt akin to the man who had taken a 'line for a walk' (as imagined by Paul Klee) in one or two simple movements of his childlike hand.

First in line is *Lion*, sketched in pen and black ink and barely recognisable as the king of beasts. The body is misshapen and lumpy

---

[98] Isobel Armstrong, *Language & Living Form In 19th Century Poetry*, 1982

[99] Tate Britain online information, 2004

and he looks more like a dog or a goat than a lion. A very young child might have drawn this. The figure is endearing. The hasty sketch suggests the lion feels out of place as Gaudier appears to have done during his short life.

Next there are *Leopards I & II* drawn in pen and blue ink. They are almost identical and look like cats with a touch of the fox in their pointed faces. One of the leopards is awake and the other has her eyes half closed, as if dozing but alert. They might be rare breeds. I imagine them being carried out of the ark on two plump cushions to please a pampered king or queen. I can hear and see them purring and preening. Their wildness has almost been tamed, but there's a warning in the eyes of the one half asleep that says, 'Don't be too sure I won't claw you if you come too close.' As a lover of cats I'm not scared. I suddenly realise, though, that these leopards of Gaudier's have no spots. Maybe he was thinking of Sophie Brzeska and himself coming out of the cold into a London society that could be equally chilly.

Third in line is *Jaguar*. She is on her own and looks more like a real animal than those who arrived before her. She is prowling and the expression on her face is mean. Like the leopards, her smaller brethren, she has no markings. She is solitary and possesses an exceptionally strong bite. Close behind her and swishing their tails, come *Pumas I & II*. They are smaller than the jaguar and their colouring is an overall tawny gold. Pumas are generally reclusive and live in mountains. Gaudier's drawings of the pumas do not look anything like the real thing I have seen on tv or in books. They are like elongated greyhounds, who have strayed a long way off their usual tracks.

The next animal, the fourth, is delightful. I warm to her straightaway, even though I have not come across her kind before and, so far as I can recall, I've never heard her name. At first I thought *Eland* was a goat but she is larger and wears a sweet expression on her small face. She looks at her audience rather bashfully, her head turned towards us over her left shoulder. She is stocky and a little cumbersome, as though she is not yet used to the tan coloured body she carries around with her on the plains of Southern Africa. She appears at ease with the long slim horns, which are elegant and suit her.

Eland is a plains antelope, a herbivore. They form herds of up to five hundred animals but are not territorial, preferring habitats with a wide variety of flowering plants such as savannah, woodlands, and open grasslands. They avoid dense forests and can trot up to twenty-two kilometres per hour indefinitely. They live between fifteen and twenty years. In captivity she may even arrive at the grand old age of twenty-five. Elands are generally placid and startle easily. They need to be careful as they are preyed upon by lions and spotted hyenas. The males are good at protecting the herd and, as the eland migrates widely in search of fertile grazing grounds, they do not establish a territory of their own. The common eland's population is decreasing (their meat is tender) but it is classified as 'Least Concern' by the International Union for Conservation of Nature.

I imagine Gaudier's eland alighting from the ark at my door. She is in a permanent state of transition from one place to another, trotting merrily along her way. As there is no fixed place she calls her own for long, there is no specific territory to be attacked or defended. She is here one day and gone the next. Elands browse on savannahs, which are located in transitional zones between forest and grassland. On a savannah the trees are widely spaced to allow the sunlight in and the grass to grow.

This animal steps out of Gaudier's sketch like an eland calf newly born: she is up and trotting with the herd a few hours after birth. Quick on her feet, despite her rather awkward body, she jumps out of the ark by the park lodge. She seems composed, even though she's the first herbivore in the line and surrounded by predators.

Next there is a great lumbering fellow, who is awkwardly seated on the ground. His head is in profile and one eye stares out of the sketch warily. The large bison has fallen over and cannot get up. He is used to wallowing in mud on an open plain and one look at the Lodge is enough for him to see he could not possibly fit in here. He could (if he chose) devour all the animals in the line without batting an eyelid.

Only the grey wolf (and then usually in a pack), the human with a gun or a grizzly bear can get the better of him and there are none of those around so far as he can see.

Where do bison live? In America mostly and some in Europe. The European kind originated in the Steppes of Central Asia. He attempts to get up but seems unable to bear his own weight. The bison reminds me of my father (his Russian father, Alexis, migrated to Britain from Central Asia) in later life, when he had put on several stone in weight. With his slim legs, the extra weight made him look top-heavy. I can see my slim young father in among the animals. He stops at the sight of the lumbering, injured bison he could not (even in his wildest dreams) imagine becoming himself. And then the figure of an ordinary middle-aged man (his more solid weight evenly distributed) appears and takes the boy's hand. At this halfway point in his life (when he was engaged in his ten year analysis with Paula Heimann) my father was (I think) confident that he would be able to deal with what life threw at him and surmount the strong tendency to melancholy that had marked him since childhood.

What a quaint gathering this is! The animals are at a loss as to what will happen next. No-one appears to be supervising them. Where are my therapist-keepers? I need to get a hold of these animals in my mind.

The animals – one lion, two leopards, one jaguar, two pumas, the eland and the bison gaze around at the green English park at my door and up into the large mature trees, where birds alight on the branches in full summer leaf. They are the six birds in Gaudier's *Studies of Birds* (c 1912-1913) sketch. They are plump and barely distinguishable as to type. The birds might all be London pigeons apart from an owl (ah, that might be one of the therapy birds) who sits on a branch, eyeing me directly, while the others are either looking down or in the opposite direction. These animals and birds, the products of Gaudier's imagination and now of mine, remind me of 'the queer-looking party' Alice comes across in among the deep strata of Lewis Carroll's Wonderland – a 'Duck and a Dodo, a Lory and an Eaglet' along with a very articulate Mouse 'who seemed to be a person of some authority among them.'[100]

What am I to make of Gaudier's gathering of animal spirits? I turn to my father's volumes for illumination. Those six birds drawn by Gaudier that I have placed in the trees facing my window remind me of something from Freud. I scan the index and find the case of Sergei Pankejeff, who is sadly still today known not by his real name but as the 'wolf man', a patient treated by Freud. The account of his treatment was written in 1914 and published in 1918 under the title, *From the History of an Infantile Neurosis*. One of the dreams he recounted to Freud has become very well-known and is published in the Standard Edition with a drawing by Pankejeff.

> *I dreamt that it was night and that I was lying in my bed. (My bed stood with its foot towards the window; in front of the window there was a row of old walnut trees. I know it was winter when I had the dream, and night-time.) Suddenly the window opened of its own accord, and I was terrified to see that some white wolves were sitting on the big walnut tree in front of the window. There were six or seven of them. The wolves were quite white, and looked more like foxes or sheep-dogs, for they had big tails like foxes and they had their ears pricked like dogs when they pay attention to something. In great terror, evidently of being eaten up by the wolves, I screamed and woke up.* [101]

The twenty-one year old Gaudier was sketching the six birds at London Zoo between 1912 and 1913 whilst Freud, in his fifties, was seeing Pankejeff (who was a few years older than Gaudier) in his consulting rooms in Vienna between 1910 and 1914. Gaudier's birds strike me as more spontaneously drawn than the wolves in Pankejeff's drawing, which are static and inert. The wolves all face the viewer whilst Gaudier's birds look in many directions and, apart from the owl, seem uninterested in the observer, as if they were getting on with their lives

---

[100] Ch 2 & 3, Lewis Carroll, *Alice's Adventures in Wonderland*, 1865

[101] Ibid, 29

– which, for the psychoanalytic patient, is the raison d'etre arrived at (hopefully) when well-being is restored.

Much has been written about Freud's interpretation of Pankejeff's dream as indicative of his patient having witnessed a 'primal scene' of his parents having sex *a tergo* at a very young age. Freud's interpretation has been disputed by many including his patient and I am, for the purposes of this book, primarily interested in my having returned to reading the case study by way of Gaudier's drawings.

Whilst Freudian analysis continues to be creative, revelatory and incisive in its establishment and exploration of the unconscious in the face of the current 'needs must' preference (in a disintegrating NHS) for short-term behavioural therapy (which has its place), the dangers of the 'interpretive' Freudian model are now being discussed by many therapists and analysts. Psychoanalytic treatment is being re-formulated as a 'listening' cure, in the course of which the patient finds, gets in touch with, her or his own words and emotions and histories, by way of the analyst holding, engaging with (often without speaking) and allowing the mind and the body/body and mind of the patient to come into play.

When I first saw Gaudier's sketches I found myself in touch with the child-self I once was. I delighted in the rawness and spontaneity of the drawing whilst my adult-self was painfully conscious of Gaudier's imminent death in the First World War. When I studied the drawings I had yet to learn more about the man himself. That is my way. I prefer to look and respond closely to pictures and words and most importantly the life I find in myself and others, before engaging more analytically and by reference to texts and contexts.

To return to Pankejeff's dream, I am struck by his recording that the season was winter, the wolves were white and that they looked more like 'foxes or sheep-dogs'. My picturing of Gaudier's birds in the park trees took place in high summer. The whiteness of the page, upon which Gaudier sketched his animals, is more like summer air within which invisibility the lines of the artist's birds are drawn. Pankejeff's description of his wolves being more like 'foxes or sheep-dogs' reminds me of the foxes I saw in the courtyard when I moved into my studio in winter. Foxes frequent this area of south east London, where there are many trees and woods in which their wildness can live and breathe.

As a child and as an adult I have related to animals, cats and dogs especially – firstly very spontaneously as a child and later as symbols of love, affection and fear. Cats were always there in my childhood and I have loved them for their cool, playful and affectionate animality. Dogs have proved more difficult and from a young age I feared the obvious sources of terror, such as German shepherd dogs, with good reason. Aged five or so I was nearly attacked by one as I walked towards a neighbour's house. The dog had threatened many children in the area and was later put down. I did, though, at the same age, love and play with Kim, the golden retriever belonging to my aunt and uncle on their Wiltshire farm.

In my late teens I had a similar dream to Sergei Pankejeff. I would dream that a wolf-like man was climbing through my bedroom window in order to attack me. The trees that I loved in our garden, which faced my window, disappeared in the face of my attacker. Still dreaming, I would scream the moment he entered the room and came toward my bed, his large shadow looming over me. Then I would jump out of bed, run to the window and pull it up, at which point I woke. The dreams stopped when I began in 1987 the long period of psychoanalytic therapy, in the course of which I discussed this dream many times.

It took me a long time to realise that I was dreaming of and fearing Andrew's epilepsy as much as I was dreaming of my brother. There was also a certain amount (never in the fullest sense) of occasional sexual involvement with my brother in my early adolescence and that reality, combined with an immense general fear of Andrew's epilepsy, was sufficient to fill me with terror.

I look out of my window now, thirty-six years after my brother's death in 1977. Gaudier's animals and birds, the eland especially, are waiting for some direction and now they all turn their heads and look toward my studio, like characters in search of an author or an analyst to help them find a story or a reason to be there, and then there is a heart-stopping moment. Watch out! Vultures overhead! One, two, three, four. I realise in time the warning is premature. Gaudier's vultures are not swooping down on their prey. They are sitting peacefully on the branches of the trees. I can even detect a slight smile on their beaks. Only the fourth is beginning to spread her wings. This book is my fourth.

In his long essay on Leonardo Da Vinci Freud explored the vulture by way of his painting, *The Virgin and Child with St. Anne* (in which the Virgin's garment reveals a vulture when viewed sideways) as 'a symbol of motherhood' deriving from Egyptian folklore: 'the vulture was regarded as a symbol of motherhood because only female vultures were believed to exist; there were, it was thought, no males of this species.' The vultures, Freud continues, were, in the absence of the male, believed to be 'impregnated by the wind' (XI, 89).[102] Da Vinci had written in the Codex Atlanticus that he had a very early memory of being visited by a vulture in his cradle. The vulture had opened his mouth with his tail and 'struck me a few times with his tail against my lips'. [103] Freud interpreted this memory as being based on the memory of sucking his mother's nipple. As an illegitimate child Da Vinci was first raised by his blood mother and then adopted by his father's wife, so he had, in effect, two mothers. The artist's preoccupation with mothers and a vulture visitation (signifying the absence of a father) were, Freud suggests, an explanation for his homosexuality.

The vultures Gaudier sketched might be male or female and they do not appear to be at all vulture-like. I have lived as if there were no men outside my father who could nurture and sustain me – as if I were a very special and impregnable child of my dreams and of psychoanalysis and of the many women who have helped me and become my friends. I have wondered if I am gay or bisexual. Now, though, my therapist is a younger male and he is helping me appreciate that maleness does not always need to be feared and can even be experienced as comforting and comfortable, nurturing and kind. And then I look again at the line

---

[102] Freud, 'Leonardo Da Vinci and a Memory of his Childhood', 88 – 89, XI (1910) ibid
[103] Ibid, 82

of animals and the birds in the trees. They are waiting for a sign to take on living forms.

These sketches of Gaudier's are like preliminary ideas and there is a hint of a suggestion, in their quick forms, that a transition is being made. Some of their bodies are misshapen. There are rare breeds and the leopards have not yet been spotted in their wild beauty. There are carnivores and herbivores co-existing, predators and their potential prey. At this moment of writing they are there for all to see without camouflage. The potential for flight and migration can be seen in the studies of birds but a halt is also signalled by the solitary owl, that wise old therapy bird, looking me in the face. Be wise and wait is her/his part stern, part friendly dictum. There will always be vultures around, ready to swoop down on the carcass of a dead animal, but surely they have no place here in this pastoral London park. The barely recognisable vultures may no longer be vultures by the morning.

I return to the figure of my inert father, a lumbering bison. He will always accompany me in one form or another and at times I shall get him back on his feet in my reveries, and then he can be at my side. Ah, there is the lovely eland. Let me remind you of her qualities: she is a herbivore and long-living; she enjoys moving in herds from one place to another and stops to browse in transitional zones, the savannahs that lie between forest and grassland. This way she escapes potential predators who like her tender meat. Above all she trots along her way.

I like to trot like the eland. I like to keep moving without settling for good. I like to take life as it comes in those threshold, transitional zones – those places between the too deep forest and the open spaces where I feel more vulnerable. At times I slow down and then sometimes I can hear the grass growing beneath my small hooves. Everywhere, though, is so busy these days, even in this pastoral south London enclave. I toss my head and take a breath. I'm not scared of the traffic.

There's one more animal just come into view. She jumps down from the van and we all turn toward her, admiring her style and panache. This animal is drawn in pen and green ink and she has a determined expression. She sits down on the grass, her paws drawn close and neatly in front of her. The whiskers are splendid, all nine of them. Here's a cat who has lived many lives and she is still on her feet, hungry for more. There is a flurry of ink strokes around her head, as though Gaudier were suggesting the aura the tiger possesses. She is the last to jump down from the van, as if waiting to make a more dramatic entrance. The tiger reminds me of my mother, who relishes life with more than a hint of the tiger in her eyes, even at the age of eighty-six years and counting.

Tigers are under threat, with 97% of wild tigers being lost in the last century. As few as 3,200 tigers exist in the wild today. In the Himalayas they have moved higher up the mountains to escape being poached. A 'tiger corridor', running along the foothills of the Himalayas from Nepal into Bhutan and Northern India, is being explored by conservationists and they have found tigers miraculously engaged in their struggle for survival.[104]

My mother is a beautiful tiger – resourceful and strong and terrible at times. She is one of the last in the 'breed' of indomitable English women, the mothers of my generation who are in their eighties and nineties today. They survived the Second World War, experienced rationing and did not have the luxury of central heating for half their lives. Some even spurn such artificial heat today. My mother, in her retirement flat, hardly ever turns on her heating. She throws open windows, even in bitter winter cold, to let the air and the elements in. These women ate what they were served and expected their children to do likewise. They knew life could throw anything at them from one day to the next. They witnessed the Holocaust and Hiroshima. They did not exhibit an air of entitlement built on castles in the air or in banks puffed up but empty of hard coin. My mother lost her first-born cub when he died, aged twenty-six, from a haemorrhage brought on by a life-time of epilepsy.

She has, though, survived and keeps enjoying the sun and the trees and the hills. She still provides home cooking for her remaining

---

[104] *Lost Land of the Tiger* (documentary), BBC1, 2010

three adult children and their children and perhaps she'll live to feed her grand-children's children. I think she can and will. She has the tiger in her so at times you need to watch out for her quick temper and at times biting sarcasm. She is, after all, hungry for life.

Gaudier's animals beside the Lodge disappear at dusk. Their temporary home is empty now but I can fill it with my magic pen. This talk of tigers is making me very hungry, even though it's only five pm and there are two full hours before my self-appointed dinner-time. I'll prepare some sea bass, pine nuts and salad today, washed down with a South American wine called *Latitude*.

SOURCES

London Zoo information
Tate Britain website

9

Van Gogh in The Stores

The Lernaean hydra with its countless flickering serpent's heads – one of which was immortal – was, as its name tells us, a water-dragon. Heracles the culture-hero, fought it by cutting off its heads; but they always grew again, and it was only after he had burnt up the immortal head with fire that he overcame the monster. A water-dragon subdued by fire – that surely makes no sense. But, as in so many dreams, sense emerges if we reverse the manifest content. In that case the hydra is a brand of fire and the flickering serpent's heads are the flames; and these, in proof of their libidinal nature, once more display, like Prometheus's liver, the phenomenon of re-growth, of renewal after attempted destruction. Heracles, then, extinguishes this brand of fire with – water.[105]

When I recently read this short essay by Freud for the first time, Van Gogh's sunflowers immediately came to mind. My mother has often recalled taking me to the National Gallery when I was five years old. A nurse was looking after Andrew and, as my brother's illness took up most of

---

[105] Freud, 'The Acquisition of Fire', 191 – 192, XXII (1932 – 1936) ibid

my mother's time, to have her to myself was a rare event.

'The first picture you noticed was the painting of sunflowers by Van Gogh!'

This was the only visit I ever made, as a child, to a gallery with my mother and I've always liked to hear her recount my rapturous response to Van Gogh's *Sunflowers* (1888), one of the four versions he painted in Arles in the South of France. The painter had gathered Provencal sunflowers in August, high summer, when the flowers were at the height of their hardiness and bloom. One of the four paintings is at the National Gallery in London, one is in Munich and one was bought by a private collector.

When my mother tells this story of the sunflowers, there has been, despite my pleasure, an undercurrent of concern. I have never actually liked sunflowers in reality or in a painting that much. They always strike me as too much 'in my face', too bright, too vigorous. I have never before, though, explored this train of thought and it strikes me that Freud's description of the hydra and Heracles 'cutting off its heads' reminds me of sunflowers and the many 'heads' Van Gogh painted. I would like to strike them all off at one fell swoop. 'Off with their heads!' I cry like the Queen of Hearts in Lewis Carroll's *Alice*. And yet the sunflowers refuse to be bowed, unless to the sun that keeps them growing. I warm to Freud's interpretation of the serpent's heads as 'flames', with Heracles finally subduing the 'water-dragon' with fire.

Andrew was a sunflower whose illness kept blossoming. No amount of medication could subdue the epilepsy, which seemed to grow back more fiercely after each and every attempt. He was Prometheus suffering on the rock, his life torn out of him day and night by the condition that never let up.

I was the sister who had all the time in the world to spare for her brother. Like Clytie in the Greek myth, I was only mortal compared with my brother turned sun-god in my eyes. In his presence I was rooted to the spot and could only follow his journey through the hours. He was so caught up inside his illness (which had an air of divinity), his sister barely existed and on his death, she was turned into a sunflower that always turned to face the sun, a picture of constancy and loyalty. And then his illness became hers after he had gone.

Van Gogh's *Sunflowers* are my brother and myself in one: fire and water, a 'water-dragon'. No-one can put out our flames, unless...unless it is a therapy-hero or more to my taste a therapy- gardener, arrived to help us out of this dilemma.

Today in *The Guardian* I read Charlotte Higgins's article entitled 'Van Gogh expert sheds new light on lost *Sunflowers* painting ', in which she recounts the recovery by Martin Bailey of 'a previously unknown 1920s print of *Six Sunflowers*', the fourth sunflower painting. He found the print in the Mushakoji Saneatsu Memorial Museum in Japan, the painting having 'met its doom on the same day that Hiroshima was destroyed, in a separate bombing attack on Ashiya.' The picture was framed in elaborate gilt and 'hung above the sofa of a wealthy collector, Loyata Yamamoto':

> **As fire engulfed the house, the large frame made the picture too heavy to rescue.**[106]

Van Gogh's four paintings of the sunflowers were *Three Sunflowers* (private collection), *Six Sunflowers* (the one destroyed in Japan), *Twelve Sunflowers* (Neue Pinakothek, Munich) and *Fifteen Flowers* (National Gallery). Now there is the print of the *Six Sunflowers* at the Mushakoji Saneatsu Memorial Museum, like a footprint of the original painting by Van Gogh. There are thirty-six sunflowers extant, one short of thirty-seven, the age of Van Gogh when he died, almost certainly shooting himself.

It is thirty-seven years since my brother, Andrew, died. I imagine him standing before Van Gogh's *Sunflowers* warming his hands at their fire – the flames of epilepsy that tortured him but did accord him the power of a devastating illness. Tall and big, Andrew, aged twenty, stood in front of the fire in the sitting-room, which he stoked

---

[106] Charlotte Higgins, 'Lost Van Gogh sunflowers bloom again', *The Guardian*, 5.9.2013

to an almighty blaze despite our protests. His enormous frame almost obscured the flames behind him. Promethean, he stood, legs astride, arms outstretched, daring us to challenge him. His smile mocked this family who cannot ease his pain, cure his epilepsy, and in his late teens Andrew began to hate us for our powerlessness as his illness grew worse.

When I see Van Gogh's *Sunflowers* at the National Gallery my eyes do not rest on them for long, although I shall keep returning to their blaze. Like Prometheus I want my brother's fire. I am reminded of the 'creature' made by Mary Shelley's Dr. Frankenstein. He was initially an inoffensive child feeding on nuts and berries but, on seeing himself in the eyes of others and in his own reflection, his grievance and rage began to grow. On his rejection by the cottagers, to whom he had lovingly attached himself, looking in on them (unseen) in the hovel annexed to their cottage, he burnt the house down and danced furiously around the cottage.

My brother had been a sensitive, lively little boy, even when racked by seizures, but by late adolescence all the joy had been knocked out of him. Like Frankenstein's 'creature' he looked at his mother, his father, his siblings and their relative 'normality' and he raged at his predicament. In the eyes of others he saw his strangeness and illness reflected. In those less enlightened times (the fifties and sixties) he was shunned by most and even his family partly turned their eyes away eventually.

The story of Richard in Stephen Poliakoff's wonderful television drama, *Perfect Strangers* (2001), tells of a boy who grows strange and of the beloved family that eventually cannot cope with where his psychosis is leading him.

I see the face of Andrew in Van Gogh's sunflowers and still cannot help turning away – I turn my head to look more comfortably at works such as some flower paintings by Winifred Nicholson I saw recently at Dulwich Picture Gallery. I was reminded by Nicholson of my father's favourite flowers – the delicate pink cyclamens that always sat on the piano in the sitting-room, lovingly tended by my father. I and my siblings brought him cyclamens in the nursing home where he died.

I wonder if my father knew that cyclamens were the favourite flower of Martha Freud (nee Bernays), the wife of Freud. [107] The cyclamen symbolically can stand for love but also for resignation and leave-taking. The symbolism suits my father very well. He was resigned in the face of Andrew's illness and in his eldest son's defiance of everything he stood for (including all 'shrinks' and 'that madman, Freud!'). Paula Heimann told him (according to my father) that he was 'committing suicide' when he decided to leave his analysis very abruptly after ten years. She was perhaps being too severe, given the many circumstances that led to my father's departure from her consulting room, the primary one being the deterioration of Andrew's illness as well as my parents' lack of the funds necessary to a full analysis. Travelling from Surrey to London five days a week also took its toll.

I have long survived both Andrew and my father, but I still shy away from the story of Van Gogh's ill health, the mental pain he was expressing when he cut off parts of his left ear. I have associated him with my brother's suffering (Van Gogh may have suffered from epilepsy) and I resist the Romantic version of the Van Gogh story, whereby creativity is linked to insanity and 'genius'. I prefer to treat Van Gogh's art as a wonderful example of the persistence of the creative mind and spirit in being able to resist debilitating distress long enough to continue his work. The thirty-six sunflowers are a triumph of endeavour against the odds.

And now another Dutchman appears at my shoulder. Frank Stoop did not buy any of Van Gogh's Sunflower paintings but he did purchase four works, which the artist painted between 1880 and 1890. Unlike the flourish of bright colours you see in *Sunflowers*, the feeling in the first two pictures is darker and more muted. I saw these pictures at the Tate Stores (on the same day as I viewed Cezanne's *The Gardener Vallier*) and was moved by the tenderness and depth in Van Gogh's art. The huge impersonal store-room became an enormous garden shed in that moment of looking. The man showing me around the stores

---

[107] Freud, 'The Material and Sources of Dreams', 169, IV (1900) ibid

seemed to sense my emotion and retreated into the shadows, allowing me to spend more private time engaging with and tending these new Van Gogh plants Frank Stoop had supplied to the Tate.

Frank bought *Thatched Roofs* (1884) from Johanna Van Gogh-Bonger, the wife of Theo Van Gogh, Vincent's brother. Johanna edited the brothers' voluminous correspondence after both had died, producing the first volume in Dutch in 1914, which ensured Vincent would enjoy fame, albeit posthumously. The pen and ink drawing depicts a group of cottages in winter at Nuenen in the province of Brabant. Van Gogh sketched the drawing very quickly to catch the light in the sepia sunset glow. The focus is on the roofs of half a dozen thatched cottages, with a bare-leaved and spindly tree in the foreground. *Thatched Roofs* possesses a closed down quality in spite of the warmish sky (maybe Dr. Frankenstein's 'creature' is lodging beneath one of those roofs and looking into the warm glow of a nearby family).

During his two year stay at Nuenen Van Gogh completed between two and three hundred works that included drawings, watercolours and oil paintings. At this stage of his career the palette he used consisted mostly of earth tones without the bright colours associated with his later work. Theo, when attempting to sell his brother's work in Paris, wrote to him that the paintings were too dark compared with the brighter Impressionist paintings being produced by his contemporaries.

Thatched Roofs reminded me of a much loved sepia photograph that can warm us in the present, despite pervasive melancholy and a density of impenetrable nostalgia. Frank also bought Van Gogh's later painting, *A Corner of the Garden of St. Paul's Hospital at St. Remy* (1889), from Johanna. In this graphite and chalk drawing I saw an intensity of pain in the 'twisted, writhing forms' of the trees, the picture's main focus. Many experts have concluded that Van Gogh painted this picture when he was staying at the hospital of St. Paul-de-Mausole, a Provencal monastery which functioned as a place of spiritual healing as early as the fourth century BC. Van Gogh committed himself to its care on the 8th May 1889 and Theo arranged for two small rooms to be used by his brother, one to be employed as a studio.

Van Gogh stayed at the hospital for a year and painted many of his most well-known works there, including *The Starry Night*. He painted the cornfields and the olive trees, along with the hospital interiors and the garden, a corner of which is the subject of the painting Frank bought.

I find this a difficult picture to engage with. It seems like the work of a disturbed child who feels cornered and I am relieved that Van Gogh left the monastery after a year. However benign an establishment may be, it is nonetheless an institution. My brother, Andrew, lived at several institutions – hospitals, homes, a shamefully named 'epileptic colony' and finally a gentle Franciscan monastery in Dorchester not long before he died. He found comfort in the West Country heartland that I think must have reminded him of our mother and her roots in Somerset. His actual home with us in the years before he died could no longer accommodate his illness.

On seeing Van Gogh's painting I was reminded of the monastery in Dorchester, my brother's temporary home. As I gazed at the picture, the technician still stood at a distance, allowing me an engagement which took about fifteen minutes but felt like hours. There is no way out in this painting. The trees are barring the way.

Van Gogh left the monastery at St. Paul-de-Mausole voluntarily and in May 1890 this disturbed and brilliant man moved to Auvers-sur-Oise, a small town to the north of Paris. On 27th July 1890, aged thirty-seven, Van Gogh died, almost certainly by his own hand. I turned away from the picture, tears in my eyes. After thirty-six years I am still mourning the brother I survived. I am mourning the child I once was and then the adult who was caught up in corners of her mind fighting the world with bare fists for her brother's life and for hers. They were twin-souls in suffering.

The other two pictures Frank bought were painted during that last fateful year of the artist's life and they are two of his most beautiful and mature works, suggesting resolution of spirit and a tangible sense of hopefulness. Hope and despair are close cousins or siblings. Had he lived, I feel Van Gogh could have gone from strength to strength despite his difficulties. He is hailed as a 'genius' today but his brilliance, coupled with a disturbed psyche, has ensured that his pain is fixed like fetish in the world's imagination.

In Auvers Van Gogh lived in a small rented room on the first floor of the Ravoux Inn near the home of Paul Gachet, a physician recommended by the Impressionist painter, Camille Pissarro. Between mid-May and the end of July he produced many paintings, several of which were of the landscape around Auvers. He wrote to his younger sister at the beginning of June, 1890: 'There are some roofs of mossy thatch here which are superb and of which I shall certainly make something.' The 'mossy thatch' is a comfortable idea, unlike the vision of neglect seen in the earlier *Thatched Roofs*. *Farms near Auvers* (1890) and *The Oise at Auvers* (1890), the two paintings Frank bought, were the paintings that emerged at this time.

In *Farms near Auvers* Van Gogh painted the houses with their thatched roofs, some dilapidated, converging toward the centre of the picture. They are in among trees and their verdant green leaves. There are wheat fields rich with harvest. The brush strokes are strong and vigorous. I studied the painting at the National Gallery recently with some students, who (knowing the story of Van Gogh's severed bits of ear but very few of his paintings apart from the *Sunflowers*) were surprised and then pleased at the hopeful tone of this late work.

Farms near Auvers reminds me of the tiny china houses my aunt Susan (Peter Stoop's wife) sent me every year on my birthday, the 21st of June. One little china house remains and lives in my kitchen today. It has a thatched roof, two front windows and a door. At the base there are two green hedges. This little china ornament, this treasured object, has travelled with me through the decades and somehow this idea of home and of its symmetry has survived, despite the other china houses all being lost along the way. The line of little houses in my aunt's gift might have made up a whole village like the one in which I now live.

Freud has written of houses symbolising the body. As a child I was not interested in dolls' houses and was always happiest in our large garden (the material reality Freud associates with the mother's body) on the outside of our home. I have in my adult life located myself primarily in my mind (which has served me very well) looking on at my body as if it were a stranger. I love the wheat fields and their harvest in *Farms near Auvers* but I am aware of the neglect inside the cottages. In more recent times my body (my maternal home) has been coming into its own. I recently went for a health check and the nurse declared that I was in 'perfect condition'. I begged to disagree. There is a way to go, I feel, but there was a spring in my step as I returned home. I felt restored.

The last of the four pictures in Frank's bequest is *The Oise at Auvers* (1890), which depicts a view across the river Oise towards the Paris road. The picture possesses an open feeling, as if Van Gogh were at this moment able to gaze around him in delight, despite his precarious health. He drew this view whilst standing on a railway embankment. His letters from Auvers suggest that he was appreciating the countryside very much.

I imagine Van Gogh standing on top of the steep embankment looking down on farmland plotted and ploughed. The old bridge at Auvers (now replaced by a modern structure) is on the right and there's a suggestion of smoke from a passing train in the bottom right-hand corner, an idea of people going somewhere. There are two figures in the foreground wheeling a barrow down a path, a child and its mother or sibling perhaps. Another figure is at work in a field. I count eight cows in the field. Eight in so many cultures is a number of hope. It has always been my favourite number. I love its roundness. Round and round the garden like a teddy bear – one step, two step, tickle you under there! My mother's voice returns to me in all its hopefulness and strength.

It is often at the point of recovery that people take their own life, as though they cannot bear to see the good health they've missed in a life-time's struggle with malaise. I have myself experienced that desire for annihilation at keen and crucial points of recovery on my therapeutic journey. A friend once asked me if I was feeling 'optimistic'. No, never optimistic, I replied. But I am hopeful. Hope does not exist on a pessimism/optimism scale. Hope simply is and it is humble.

The small figure of hope remained in a corner of Pandora's box after being opened and its sorrows released into the world. In writing of hope I am reminded of a poem I wrote in 1997. This was one of the first poems to be published in *The Rialto* but I chose not to include it in my collection, *In Slow Woods* (2011), as I was unsure of its quality or import at the time.

Dream

The buildings were baroque, slow-moving problems
in the middle of a partly-lit long day:

I did not dream of roses, only touched deep maroon
high-colouring an awkward bridge –

a sapphire studded horse was nudging me
to hold one small detail,
eye-still clarities to test my hand
on his garnet halting-rein;

then the sun arrived on my bare back
and shoulders, heating one elegant
but riding-mournful girl
fed hungry-warm on pine-nuts
from some memory stored near

and trembling awake at early dawn

the jewels fell upon a sandy boulevarde
and I cried to remember
their slow pattern
one by one.

I hesitate to analyse this poem that emerged when I began (for the first time in my life) to write poetry in my late forties, but surely I was suggesting (without knowing) the figure of Clytie, the mortal in the myth who can only love the sun-god, Helios. She cannot 'dream of roses': her sole companion is the 'sun', in whose sole honour she may flower. She is lost in reverie for those who have passed. Her condition is hyphenated, joined at the hip to the dead. She is pining away. I take that girl by the hand and speak kind words to her.

'Look, the buildings around you in London (where you really do live and work and have your being) are solid structures. Let us cross the bridge together with our sturdy (do look at him) rather glamorous horse – what a picture he is! He will not harm you. You might even take his rein, if he threatens to run away or go too fast. When you are fully awake the picture will still be there. Your dreams are yours. They are not your brother's. They are not your father's. Yes, I know your Dad was rather over-full of Freud and all those phallic 'flickering serpent's heads' that might be cut off at any moment, but then the sixties was a very exciting time for psychoanalysis.

Come, take my hand. We can lift our feet and take the first steps together.'

SOURCES

Tate website

10

Pictures by English Artists

A castle by the sea; later it was no longer immediately on the sea, but on a narrow canal leading to the sea. The Governor was a Herr P. I was standing with him in a big reception room – with three windows in front of which there rose buttresses with what looked like crenellations. I had been attached to the garrison as something in the nature of a volunteer naval officer. We feared the arrival of enemy warships, since we were in a state of war. Herr P. intended to leave, and gave me instructions as to what was to be done if the event that we feared took place. His invalid wife was with their children in the threatened castle. If the bombardment began, the great hall was to be evacuated. He breathed heavily and turned to go; I held him back and asked him how I was to communicate with him in case of necessity. He added something in reply, but immediately fell down dead. No doubt I had put an unnecessary strain upon him with my questions. [...] I was standing at the window, and observing the ships as they went past. They were merchant vessels rushing past rapidly through the dark water [...] Then my brother was standing beside me and we were both looking out of the window at the canal. At the sight of one ship we were frightened and cried out: 'Here comes the warship!' But it turned out that it was only the same

*ships that I already knew returning. There now came a small
ship, cut off short, in a comic fashion, in the middle. On its deck
some curious cup-shaped or box-shaped objects were visible.
We called out with one voice: 'That's the breakfast-ship!'*[108]

I stand in *my* 'castle'/studio beside my three windows, looking out
at the trees/the sea outside, and then suddenly the 'castle' is no
longer in Dulwich Village. I lift it up in my mind, like a child's toy,
to place beside the bridges that span the Thames at Embankment
tube station – the old structure of Hungerford Bridge flanked by the
two Golden Jubilee footbridges, those elegant structures completed
in 2002 and named in celebration of the fiftieth anniversary of Queen
Elizabeth II's accession. Unlike the 'narrow canal' in Freud's dream, the
Thames is wide and promises a relatively easy route toward the oceans.

I have grown very 'attached' to the figure at my side: the spirit of
my father (via Freud) ('the Governor') who was at a psychoanalytic helm
when he directed the Paddington Day Hospital for nine years in the
sixties. I envied those patients of his in their group analytic sessions
which, according to Jenny Diski (who was a patient at the hospital),[109]
were very enjoyable and creative. My father always returned home
from his sessions, full of good humour. I am the 'volunteer naval
officer' at my father's side, lapping up any of his ideas that come my
way. In a small commuter belt Surrey village psychoanalysis was mostly
very 'foreign' in the ears of stockbrokers and builders, lawyers and
accountants, and even if neighbours read a little about the practice
in newspapers, such rummaging around in the mind was suspicious,
metropolitan, Jewish. 'We feared the arrival of enemy warships' and
then my father falls down dead, like the Governor, and I am left on my
own to defend psychoanalysis in the twenty-first century.

'No doubt I had put an unnecessary strain upon him with my
questions.' My thirst to know more of his practice may have grated on
his ears as he sank further into depression in later life. I reminded him

---

[108] Freud, 'Affects in Dreams', 463 – 464, V (1900 – 1901) ibid

[109] Jenny Diski, *The Sixties* (2010)

perhaps too much of the berth he had once secured in London with Paula Heimann and at the Institute of Psychoanalysis. Even though I am not an analyst or therapist myself, a great deal that I hold dear is here in my studio that I have located inside the psychoanalytic 'castle' and I am beginning to realise that I am prepared to defend this secure hold. Psychoanalysis is, at the current time, in a state of siege. It is under attack from the medical world (where CBT is the order of the day) and from a world that flinches from 'depth' psychology, let alone psychoanalysis. Many of our ideas, though, are actually common currency: the existence of the 'unconscious', the 'psychopathology of everyday life', the idea of darker regions of the mind. Psychoanalytic ideas are embedded in our culture and in our history, but its spirit is currently embattled. Ever hopeful, I have no doubt the practice will be respected in good time and that in the future people with little funds may also benefit from its practice.

And then 'my brother was standing beside me'. Andrew is here beside the three bridges spanning the river. He joins me in the psychoanalytic endeavour. The twenty-six year old spirit of my brother lives on and is more genial now that he has escaped the poor, racked body/mind that was his vessel in life. He no longer envies me bitterly for my relative 'normality' and robust health. We can even celebrate the building of these two new bridges over the course of the years, taking us into a future that has yet to disclose itself. The old bridge, our father and his work, is still there and we stand one each side of him. We are both feeling very hungry. Our mother and the spirit of our grandmother appear at our side. They are not 'invalid' as in Freud's dream, but very strong and in robust health. My grandmother, Dr. Hazel Chodak-Gregory, was a paediatrician at the Royal Free Hospital (where there is a plaque commemorating her work), one of the second wave of women doctors to enter into medicine. My mother, Dinah Gregory, also possesses a pioneering spirit and has had a vision of her family cutting strong figures in the world.

Andrew and I look at the two women, expecting food, but they are both tired of all the giving they have undertaken in their lives, and suddenly my mother claps her hands and then Hazel with her.

'There's the breakfast-ship!'

Andrew has a basket from which he unpacks blue and white striped cups and saucers and plates, along with cutlery, salt and pepper. He unfolds a little table and two chairs and sets them by the bridge in anticipation of breakfast. I smile at him. My brother, for the first time in my life, is inviting me to share a meal with him. In life Andrew liked to play at having meals on his own. There was no question that his little sister would be allowed to join him. My brother was like the mad hatter in *Alice* and Alice was not welcome. Andrew mostly only tolerated me if I became part of or reflected his troubled psyche: as a live girl in good health I was always going to be an intrusion. But now, we are about to enjoy some breakfast together. Hurry up little ship! We're starving.

As the small breakfast-ship comes closer we see there is a short squat figure on board. He is waving a bright red handkerchief but it is unclear whether he is waving with joy or is on the verge of collapse. Now the ship is close to the Embankment and I can see the man (who might be young, middle-aged or old) is smiling broadly. He is not drowning, only rather hot with all the bailing out he has had to do. And then I recognise my paternal grandfather, Dr. Alexis Chodak-Gregory, the subject of my earlier book, *The Sound of Turquoise*. He was one of those people who, in the early to mid-twentieth century, appeared to need no introduction. A roguish Russian émigré, he had taken London by storm as a young man newly qualified in medicine (at Edinburgh University) and had lived life to the hilt, as though there never had been any tomorrow.

Less than a year after leaving Scotland, Chodak's motorbike was a regular sight outside Bay House, 4 Heath Street, Hampstead. [...] The dashing Alexis embodies the spirit of Morfydd Owens [a young Welsh composer] Bohemia. Theirs was an intense relationship which, like her later affair with Ernest Jones [who she would marry] moved on apace. Indeed Alexis was Morfydd's most serious suitor before marriage. [110]

---

[110] Rhian Davies, *Morfydd Owen. A Life in Pictures*, 1994

My grandfather had many affairs by all accounts and would go on to fall passionately in love with and marry my grandmother, Hazel (nee Cuthbert), in 1916.

While he is tethering the breakfast-ship to the quayside, I will provide you with a brief introduction to Alexis. Circa 1904, at the age of fourteen or so, he had fled his Central Asian home in Tashkent when he and his aristocratic Russian family were lined up (most probably by local tribes-men reclaiming their land from the Russians who had invaded Tashkent in 1864) on the farmland of their dacha and executed. According to the story Alexis told his friends and family in England, the gunmen missed him in the line-up. He managed to escape by train on the newly extended railway line in Tashkent and make his way to Scotland, where he went on to study medicine. His imagined escape is recounted in *The Sound of Turquoise*, the 'turquoise' of the title referring to the domes of the mosques he glimpses from the train as he leaves Tashkent.

In 1949, thirty years after his marriage to Hazel and the birth of my father, Basil, in 1920, Alexis fled another scene of high drama. Having established himself as a very successful doctor in London and as a landowner, farmer, art collector and exhibitor at the first Aldeburgh Festival (involving a friendship with Benjamin Britten), he had gone spectacularly bankrupt, having led the life of a bon viveur way beyond his means. As though the past were continuing to haunt him, he metaphorically 'killed' off his family, the 'dear circle of three' my father (an only child) cherished, along with the rich and cultured life he and they had established. He also revealed, to the devastation of Hazel and my father (in his late twenties and freshly qualified in medicine), that he possessed a second family in the wings (a 'mistress' and two children), whom he had supported for many years in a separate establishment. Hazel and my father left him and he fled from England with his second family, returning two years later in the custody of police officers.

Alexis never talked of his Russian family background, according to my parents and the second family I traced, met and continue to meet with great pleasure. That terrible trauma of loss seems to have clouded his better judgement and he was continuing to live as though he were an exceedingly rich Russian aristocrat owning vast tracts of land and priceless works of art. I have tried to find out more about his actual family but have drawn a blank. The closest I have got is discovering there was a Grand-Duke Nikolai (a Romanov) who, in photographs of him as a child and as a man, looks uncannily like my father and also my nephew, Oscar. Nikolai was exiled to Tashkent after stealing his mother's jewels in Moscow and went on to atone for that misdemeanour by initiating a series of building works and establishing institutions in Tashkent, including an art gallery that was filled with a collection he amassed. He was the only Romanov to be accorded a state funeral by the Bolshevik authorities. He had several mistresses dotted about Tashkent, including a Cossack woman he built a castle for. She was very short and he was very tall. Alexis, my grandfather, was very short and my grandmother, Hazel, very tall, so I have imagined there is a 'Cossack' Romanov strain in my blood.

The spirit of Alexis has managed to secure the breakfast-ship beside the bridges and is now unpacking the 'cup-shaped or box-shaped objects' Andrew and I imagine is breakfast. To our surprise, though, the objects are pieces of art neatly packaged in boxes or wrapped in strong brown paper – vases, containers, ashtrays and the like. Our grandfather explains that these are the pieces he had managed to salvage from 'the wreck of my life, my children'.

In the analysis of his dream, Freud refers to the German word, 'Schiffbruch', meaning 'ship-break'. He then links the idea of a shipwreck to the word 'breakfast' meaning 'breaking fast'.

My grandfather was, in this light, involved in salvaging precious objects from the wreckage he had brought to his new English families (mirroring the wreckage in his homeland) whilst conveying to us the idea of 'breakfast' – the new beginning he strongly believed would emerge in the wake of any storm. As if by Cossack magic a full English breakfast appears on the table on which Andrew has laid one of our mother's checked tablecloths, so we sit down and eat. When we have finished Alexis, having stacked up all his art by the steps up to one of the footbridges, tells us a story.

'Once upon a time I owned a great painting by John Constable called *The Marine Parade and Old Chain Pier, Brighton.* The master painted it in 1827 and the picture was of a great storm at sea!'

I imagined the storm raging and the chains of the pier rattling. I liked the idea of a 'chain pier' which made me think of daisy chains.

'I owned one hundred and thirty-six paintings and drawings by John Constable and Thomas Gainsborough and Thomas Girtin and I even owned one by the great J.M.W. Turner! I fell in love with these pictures of England, the country that has welcomed me to her shores so kindly. I had them all hanging in a suite of gallery rooms in one of my houses – pictures of villages and farms, churches and trees, and there was one of an old bridge at Shrewsbury by Richard Wilson. There were sailing boats on the river and figures on the bank, with a view of a castle in the background. I especially loved that picture by Richard Wilson. The people at Sotheby's, a great auction house in London, said to me that it was an incredible collection! They sold all my pictures on the 20th July 1949.[111] What a sad day that was! I fled the country with my other family and I'm very sad to tell you that I left Hazel and Basil (your dear father) 'high and dry' as they say.'

He patted our heads and smiled ruefully.

'You see, my children, I have salvaged a few pieces from the wreckage and we can all begin again!'

And then the spirit of irrepressible Alexis dissolved in air, along with the spirit of my happier brother. I alone remained beside the three bridges. With the help of Freud I had conjured a 'breakfast-ship' into my existence. I am in the process of beginning to reach the end of my book. I have, in the course of the narrative, established many 'chains' of association which I hope will prove strong. The three bridges I look up at from the Embankment are pretty solid. Bridges span something – a road or in this case a river. They hold the promise of taking you from here to there or there to here. The chain pier Constable painted juts out into the sea, going nowhere.

---

[111] See Appendix

I saw another version of *Chain Pier* in 2006 (that *annus mirabilis* for pictures in my mind) when I visited *The Great Landscapes: Constable*, an exhibition at Tate Britain of Constable's 'six footers', some of them displayed next to his smaller completed sketches in oils of the same subject. *Chain Pier* was exhibited beside its earlier oil sketch. I loved the sketch, with its freer, looser brushstrokes and more concentrated intensities of colour. The sky was a brighter turquoise-pink than the darker green-blue of the bigger picture. The sketch felt watery, fresh, and had a bracing, drenched quality compared with what I saw as the more melancholy, louring atmosphere of the finished work.

The sketch set beside its established relation opened a door in my imagination. I began to see my grandfather as a buoyant figure who survived bankruptcy. In the presence of this much freer oil sketch, I see a brighter, unfinished version of my grandfather. A short squat child-like man, he was, by all accounts, a great favourite in many circles (if not (finally) in that special circle of three he had for a long while stayed inside). After being declared bankrupt he spent a few months in Brixton Prison between 1951 and 1952 but, with the help of his patients and friends, including his art dealers, the Agnew family, Alexis was acquitted and freed. He re-established his medical practice (treating rheumatic conditions whilst singing the folk tunes of his homeland for his patients' pleasure) on a more modest scale and this work flourished until his death in his early seventies.

I look more closely at the picture on a postcard of the established oil painting at the Tate, realising there are many more of Constable's trademark dabs of life-affirming red than I'd noticed before – the scene is less doom-laden than busy with the lives of the fishermen and also of the fashionable visitors to Brighton, a newly established seaside resort at that period. At the edge of the white-tipped waves there are the two women walking and talking and enjoying the scene. The one with the umbrella up is wearing a red shawl. There's a red bow of a boat and a tiny bit of red to suggest the man on board. There are touches of red on the foreshore and in the far background close to the Marine Parade. There is a red capped fisherman and his mongrel sitting higher up the beach in the foreground.

I hold the card up to the mid-morning light. The picture is not a storm-filled absence after all. It is a painting brimful of people and boats, the large settlement of Brighton and a sea that teems with energy and vitality. The white horse being ridden into the sea is a sign of rescue (should that be needed) and the man holding a telescope is a coastguard. He can see an end to the tempest in sight. There is no need to panic. The women at the edge of the waves are unperturbed and normal life will resume shortly.

Carlos Peacock, author of *John Constable: the Man & his Work*, 1965, wrote to Benjamin Britten in 1962:

> Dear Ben,
>
> We were very sorry to read in the paper that you are still having shoulder trouble. Do hope that a good rest in the Suffolk air will put you to rights. I thought I might drop over to Aldeburgh one of these days to see you. I don't want to be a nuisance, but I should like very much to reproduce two of your pictures in my Constable book – the little seapiece Dr Gregory gave you [...]
>
> Yours
> Carlos Peacock [112]

My grandfather ('Dr Gregory') had gifted Britten a 'little seapiece'. I have not been able to find out which painting this was but the idea of its modesty and smallness contrasts nicely with the sublime storm of *Chain Pier*. His friend of those early Aldeburgh days, 'Ben' Britten, signed three opera scores with little personal notes to my grandfather (*Peter Grimes*, *The Rape of Lucretia* and *Albert Herring*). I am in the process of offering the scores to the Britten-Pears Library at Aldeburgh where they should be safe from any future storms. A memorial holding of my father's papers (prepared by myself) has recently appeared online at the Institute of Psychoanalysis archive. Neither of his parents had supported

---

[112] Letter from Carlos Peacock to Benjamin Britten, 9th September, 1962, Britten-Pears Library

him in going into psychiatry, feeling it was less manly than a medical field concerning itself primarily with the body. I hope, on reflection, they would have been proud of their son's psychoanalytic legacy.

I must return to the Tate soon and see *Chain Pier* again – take in the fish spilling from a creel – the anchors and balks of timber in the foreground, the work on shore that continues, the connections and re-connections that I keep making and re-making in my engagement with this picture. When I have re-visited Tate Britain I shall take the boat to Tate Modern, metaphorically moving from the past into a more unknown present and future. I must go and see the recently opened Malevich exhibition.[113] The Dutchman Frank Stoop would surely have loved his bold 'Suprematist' art whilst my Russian grandfather would probably have shied away from such startling modernism, preferring the Romantic English landscapes that became his surrogate mother-soul in her absence.

One of the most heart-breaking and compelling moments in twentieth-century literature is to be found in Kazuo Ishiguro's important novel, *The Remains of the Day* (1989). It is the point at which Stevens, the butler, meditates on the life he has spent in service to an aristocrat, who in latter years had aligned himself with the Nazis in the run up to the Second World War. Stevens sits on a pier, near the conclusion of the novel, wondering aloud to a stranger whether his whole life has been a waste. The reader, when the stranger offers Stevens a handkerchief, realises with a jolt that the butler is crying. There is no high drama at this moment, simply exquisite pain – the pain of many who have lived too long in service to an idea that has proved stronger than the desires of their own private selves.

My grandfather was (I believe) driven by an idea of his past that destroyed the maternal castles full of healing and art he built in England. He did, though, re-build his life on a much more modest scale. He continued to live (within limits) as did my father, even though

---

[113] I have visited this exhibition since completing *The Studio* and a card of Malevich's 'The Woodcutter' (1912) (the depiction of a peasant woman) is on one of my studio walls, a picture of strength & modernity

he broke off his analysis and depression eventually got the better of him. The paternal line is secure if badly fractured at certain points. I believe my father died knowing this work of reparation, albeit very imperfect, had been partially secured. My paternal line is full of doctors and I am a doctor of poetry, a reader of my father's Freud and a patient in psychoanalysis. Life continues in this rich and nourishing vein.

SOURCES

Gill Gregory, *The Sound of Turquoise*, recounts the semi-fictionalised story of my grandfather's bankruptcy. The Britten-Pears Library has created a holding for my book in among the volumes on John Constable.

See Appendix for: Sotheby's *Sale Catalogue,* Wednesday, 20th July, 1949 and a list of the paintings by John Constable he exhibited at the first Aldeburgh Festival in 1948.

11

A Studio in Paris

The other symbol I want to talk to you about is that of the bridge [...] First it means the male organ, which unites the two parents in sexual intercourse; but afterwards it develops further meanings which are derived from this first one. In so far as it is thanks to the male organ that we are able to come into the world at all, out of the amniotic fluid, a bridge becomes the crossing from the other world (the unborn state, the womb) to this world (life); and, since men also picture death as a return to the womb (to the water), a bridge also acquires the meaning of something that leads to death, and finally, at a further remove from its original sense, it stands for transitions or changes in condition generally. [114]

I t is, of course, also 'thanks' to the mother's life-sustaining womb that we are able 'to come into the world at all, out of the amniotic fluid' and the desire to return to the womb may not necessarily signify a 'picturing' of death. That desire may involve metaphorically the need for more sustenance, more safety and more comfort before entering into the many perils of life in the outside world. We walk in

---

[114] Freud, 'Revision of Dream Theory', 24, XXII (1932 – 1936) ibid

and out of 'wombs' on a daily basis – my studio, my college, my friends' homes, picture galleries might all be read as versions of the woman's body (as Freud has suggested) and of the womb. Freud's idea of the bridge's phallic symbolism is wonderfully 'pregnant' with meaning. Suddenly my three bridges spanning the Thames in the previous chapter acquire further significance. I would suggest, though, that the bridges could be read as an idea of 'intercourse' itself rather than of the 'male organ' alone, the intercourse that unites (in that moment) and takes its course between either side of the river.

In that moment of creative and hopefully productive coming together any 'water under the bridge' is forgetful and dissolves over-weaning individual egos (male and female): in that moment of connectedness that takes place between man and woman, woman and man, past histories and past selves may be forgotten and (to that extent) the bridge, the intercourse, exists as an idea beyond time and mortality until the moment of arrival. The three bridges (one old bridge in between two new ones) I have discussed might also represent an idea of my old self being restored by my past and present therapists – a younger man and an older woman coming together metaphorically to help me span this moment of transition.

Yesterday my sister, Liz, and my two young nephews, Oscar and Pablo (aged eleven and nine), visited my studio where we improvised meals at my father's old card table, which I had restored. I laid one of my mother's old but pristine tablecloths on my father's table. The blue and white check proved cheerful. We visited the park and took a boat on the small lake and tomorrow we plan to play table tennis on the tables in the park. On the lake Oscar and Pablo took the helm, pushing the pedals and steering together, whilst Liz and I lay back, newly christened ladies of leisure at one moment until we crashed into some overhanging branches the next. We messed about on the lake for half an hour, laughing and scolding the boys for misleading us at times. We visited the shops in the village and then watched Denzel Washington in *Deja Vu*, a film released in 2006, a year after Hurricane Katrina devastated New Orleans and the year I visited many of the paintings in this book.

The film begins with a pleasure ship in New Orleans being blown up and, in the reconstruction and investigation of the crime, Washington (a firearms & explosives agent) explores the past that is re-enacted and revisited by way of new state-of-the-art technology that can return him to the scene of the crime as if in the present tense. He time travels and is able to save New Orleans from the explosion and finally the girl (one of the victims) he fell in love with when first visiting the past.

Half-way through the film Liz, Pablo and I visited the picture gallery nearby, leaving Oscar to watch *Deja Vu*.

Our visit lasted for about twenty minutes as the gallery was closing, but we managed to select some favourite pictures of flowers and boats, families and beaches, from the *Art and Life* exhibition of paintings by the married couple, Ben and Winifred Nicholson. On our return Oscar tracked back the film to where we had left off, happy to study more of the complicated plot-line. At eleven he is becoming very interested in film and its take on life. Our day arrived at a happy end with watching the FA Cup Final between Argentine and Germany from Brazil but we found ourselves barely aware of the tv, preferring to eat and talk, squabble and joke among ourselves. The high drama played out on screen in 'the beautiful game' could not compete with the ordinary pleasures of a family getting together in the small playground of my studio.

In this book I began with Landseer's picture of animals gathered in a tent and then moved into J.F. Lewis's courtyard in Cairo. I have taken my reader into the hold of a ship from Africa, where a small zebra is being carried to a new country. I have visited the Tate archive and its box files to meet up with Frank Stoop, who stands in a photograph before a summer pavilion from the past. In the Tate Stores I have come face to face with some of the paintings he loved and then bequeathed to the Tate. The room in my father's Surrey nursing home has also been revisited and, in this moment of recalling my father, I look out at the Lodge by the park gates, where Gaudier's animals assembled and resembled my family. There is quite a lot going on in this book full of pictures and I hope I have constructed plenty of bridges to make the transition from one to the other and back again.

The small gallery/womb next door is exquisite and sustaining. When I visited with Liz and Pablo, it was buzzing with but not too full of life. I have arrived at the last chapter, the eleventh, which will be followed by an Afterword. Eleven plus one afterword makes twelve. This reminds me of Freud's twenty-four volumes that have accompanied me on my journey in this studio turned time machine. This founding father of psychoanalysis has given me a great deal to think about as I've scanned his thoughts. He is there in my imagination night and day, 24/7. I write by day and dream, rest and lay relatively fallow by night. Sometimes I have disturbing dreams and sleep is fitful, but there are no nightmares now as there were for much of the first half of my life.

The seeds of *The Studio* began to be sown over twenty years ago when I first came upon Dulwich village and its gallery. Over the next couple of decades my sister Liz (who lived in East Dulwich and then Camberwell during that period) and I would meet in the village regularly, a mid-way point between her home to the east and mine to the west on the Clapham-Brixton borders. After my niece, Lucy, was born in 1996 she and my brother, Robert, would also visit the gallery with me. I remember Lucy crawling, toddling and running around the gallery garden and in among the trees and sculptures exhibited there. She would touch and trace the sculptures with her small hands, wishing perhaps that they would come alive. Inside the gallery she roamed freely, a child of art without knowing it. Her favourite picture was Guido Reni's tortured *St Sebastian* (1620). Lucy would point at the picture, giggling, loving the shock she gave herself and us.

I visited the gallery last year with Lucy, who had just turned seventeen, and this time her favourite picture was Meindert Hobbema's *Wooded Landscape with a Water-mill* (early 1660s), a lovely rich landscape with an overarching, protective tree leaning over the water and cottages. The painting reminds me of Constable's pictures of Suffolk and also of John Frederick Lewis's *The Courtyard*.[115] Lucy's imagination can now accommodate and enjoy more 'down to earth'

---

[115] See Ch 2

pictures, that do not possess the 'shocks' childhood craves and fears in equal measure. The picture gallery is (in the moment of visiting) our home from home and sometimes a nurturing 'womb'.

Over the years and with the support of a substantial Heritage Lottery grant, the gallery has flourished. Enlarged by its beautiful extension and ceiling to floor glass windows so you can see inside and out, it has become a very lively hub of art and people of all ages, as it was in the early nineteenth century. The small Georgian gallery was much loved by Victorians such as Robert Browning, Charles Dickens and John Ruskin. They would meet friends, tramp in the meadows (now Dulwich Park) and visit the gallery.

Living so close to this house full of pictures feels as though a part of myself has fallen into place. In November 2012 I moved from chaotic, creative and head-spinning Clapham – a crowded, urban place of busy hubs. There is a convergence of roads by the dome of Clapham Common tube station and also at the domed bandstand that survives as a lyrical, nostalgic point on the common in among the trees and roads that criss-cross the green. At these two domes people from all corners of the world meet and disperse and (if they are lucky) find themselves. Clapham became a dangerously over-full 'womb' for me, though, from which I needed to emerge.

In this place of perpetual movement and change I began in the early 1990s to make some sense of my life. In Clapham I found my disorientation mirrored and held in a place of multiple directions. Depression was my constant companion (it had been since I was a child of ten) and to get through each day, without escaping somewhere else to begin yet again, was sapping and time-consuming.

There I stayed, though, and went on to study for a doctorate and write three books, including *The Sound of Turquoise*, which has a picture of myself as a child standing beside the bandstand on the cover. The dark grey clouds persisted but began slowly and surely to lift, with the help of my therapist, who worked so hard and with such patience to secure my sanity through those terribly difficult years.

Despite my successes, I continued to feel very unclear as to where I was going. I did not want a full time academic career: I was not strong enough for its rigours and also wished to write at my own pace so as to discover what forms writing might take. Thankfully in 1997 I was offered some part-time lecturing at The University of Notre Dame in central London and I am still working there very happily (for half the week) after sixteen years.

Here in this south London village I have arrived at a relatively tranquil spot full of trees and small shops and the gallery and me. Here I can grow still and become more alive with possibilities than I have ever felt before. I find myself moving, making transitions in my mind, at a quicker pace in the care of my Italian, Mancunian therapist and in a quieter state of mind I am able to collect my thoughts with some sense of Wordsworth's idea of 'tranquillity' (although the Lakes poet would have found today's Dulwich very noisy with its constant traffic and crowds in the park at weekends). Here I find myself hungry for pictures that play in and nourish my mind.

Over the summer of 2013 I visited an exhibition, *A Crisis of Brilliance, 1908-1922*, at the picture gallery. I dropped by and into the gallery's halls and alcoves as if I were a member of the family come downstairs from her bedroom to take her place in a beautiful drawing-room. This temporary exhibition occupied the long corridor space that lines the back wall of the gallery. The rather 'phallic' space adjoins the main gallery or womb and I can move between them.

A Crisis of Brilliance tells the story of five young British artists and the works they painted before, during and after the First World War up to 1922, two years after my father was born in Bloomsbury in 1920. It was a fascinating exhibition and I was particularly struck by the work of Christopher R. W. Nevinson (known as C.R.W. Nevinson), whose father was a journalist and a war correspondent in Gallipoli during the First World War. The painter's mother, Margaret Wynne Jones, was a leading member of the Women's Freedom League, founded in 1907.

Their son, Christopher, grew up in a lively Hampstead home, which he describes in his wonderfully titled autobiography, *Paint and Prejudice* (1938), as a hub of radical activity, 'a meeting-place for

French, Germans, Finns, Russians, Indians, Colonials, professional Irishmen, and Suffragettes'.

After training at the Slade School of Art in London, Nevinson travelled to Paris and immersed himself in art and the Bohemian demi-monde – a world of studios in Montmartre and Montparnasse, where young artists were emulating the work of 'Post-Impressionist' painters such as Paul Cezanne, Vincent Van Gogh and Henri Matisse – the painters Frank Stoop admired so much.

In 1911, aged twenty two, Nevinson shared a studio for a while with the Italian painter, Amedeo Modigliani, who was to die tragically in 1920, aged thirty-five, from tuberculosis. Nevinson disliked the posthumous romantic myth of Modigliani as a dissipated artist. 'He was kind, constant, correct, and considerate: a bourgeois Jew,' and his friend for nine years. He died, Nevinson writes, not from dissipation but in the 'influenza scourge' after the war, his lungs weakened by a 'German gas' attack when serving in the French Foreign Legion. Whatever the precise truth of Modigliani's life and sad, early death, Nevinson was a loving friend.

Today Nevinson is most well-known for his superb paintings of the machinery of war (ahead of their time and much derided by critics initially) such as *La Mitrailleuse* (The Machine-Gun) (1915) and *La Patrie* (The Fatherland) (1916), the latter bought by the novelist, Arnold Bennett, in 1916 when Nevinson had his first one man show at the Leicester Galleries in London. As an official war artist Nevinson had witnessed the horrors of the First World War (in which both my grandfathers fought and won the Military Cross and both my grandmothers served on the front lines as a doctor and nurse), which led to his retreat from the Futurist aesthetic of dynamism and violence he had espoused before the war.

His lesser-known paintings of modernity, though, deserve a much wider audience. They might be viewed today as contemporary pieces. Nevinson's *The Viaduct at Issy-les-Moulineaux* (1913) could be the work of a twenty-first-century artist relieved to find that painting, even representational painting, is at last (after years of conceptual art) being recognised as a valid and enduring art form. My response on seeing this picture for the first time was, 'This reminds me of a Monopoly board with its little red hotels and the four stations, Liverpool Street, Fenchurch Street, Marylebone Street and King's Cross.' I enjoyed the playfulness that was so evident in the painting.

Nevinson's picture is of a steam train puffing its way over the French viaduct at Issy-les-Moulineaux , a suburb south-west of Paris. The 'moulineaux' are named after the windmills that had once stood there before the town became a beacon of modernity, hosting the beginning of the Paris to Madrid air race in 1911 and the home of Avions Voison, an automobile manufacturers, in the 1920s. Today it is a centre of telecommunications. *The Viaduct at Issy-les-Moulineaux* conveys a sense of the train's dynamic, 'phallic' energy whilst also being a childlike depiction of confident (if naive) modernity steaming onward to the centre of Paris I imagine. This is a pre-war painting, a flourish of good humour before the First World War began. P.G. Konody, critic for *The Observer*, disliked what he refers to as 'the elimination of atmosphere'[116] in the painting and G.K. Chesterton dismissed 'Mr Nevinson and the Futurists' in *The Illustrated London News* as 'having never seen a fact before in their lives':

> *Have you ever seen a fellow fail at the high jump because he had not gone far enough back for his run? That is Modern Thought. It is so confident of where it is going that it does not know where it comes from.*[117]

That is precisely what I like about the *Viaduct* painting. Nevinson possessed an international and metropolitan perspective on a transition being made from the nineteenth to the twentieth century. *The Manchester Courier* described him as 'among pioneers of painting'.[118] I like to think he was even humorously pointing the way for himself

---

[116] P.G. Konody, *The Observer*, 26 January 1913

[117] G.K. Chesterton, *The Illustrated London News*, 11 July 1914

[118] *The Manchester Courier*, 13 June 1914

and his fellow artists in Paris – suggesting that they may sometimes, in their naivety, be tilting at windmills (for les Moulineaux read the Moulin Rouge) in their small coteries. The train becomes (for me) 'the little train that could' from the story my mother read me in childhood. In the presence of this painting I hope I myself can make a transition from a more 'artful' world into one of a more full-blooded reality. I think I can. I think I can, chugs the little train. Now the words have changed, 'I feel I can. I feel I can.' [119]

Nevinson's *Le Vieux Port* (1913-14) is another work that depicts a child-like vision of modernity at work in his depiction of the arrival of a red-funnelled ship in the busy harbour of Boulogne. The port and its workers, the red-roofed hotels, the shafts and ladders, are almost imploding: the structures, figures and equipment threaten to fall over like a child's brick castle onto the vessel that (against the odds) stays afloat. The picture reminds me a little of Turner's great painting, *The Fighting Temeraire* (1839), in which the old warship is being tugged down the Thames to the breaker's yard by a little steamboat. Old and new go hand in hand, with modernity leading the way – Turner is more Romantic and appears more conflicted about the new industrial Victorian age, whilst twentieth-century Nevinson joyfully celebrates the difficult balancing act of encompassing tradition and a new style within one frame, holding them together with a wry and affectionate smile. Freud's little 'breakfast ship', arriving in the twenty-first century with the spirit of Alexis on board, comes to mind.

Walking around the exhibition, it was Nevinson's paintings that I found most arresting in among wonderful works by Dora Carrington, Paul Nash, Mark Gertler, David Bomberg and Stanley Spencer to name a few. The First World War and its destructive new armaments undermined a more hopeful picture of modernity but, unlike some of his fellow artists, Nevinson did not after the war paint (in nostalgic longing) pastoral scenes of the English countryside. Instead, he continued to signal the transition to modernity. On a visit to New York in the spring

---

[119] See p. 15

of 1919, a year after the war came to a bloody and exhausted close, Nevinson understandably embraced a city far away from Europe and its horrors. His dry-point etching, *Temples of New York* (1919), is a quiet celebration of tall buildings, a view from a skyscraper, showing the spire of Grace Church, Broadway and East 10th street. Nevinson's imagination is wonderfully 'phallic' in the most creative sense of the word.

I have not yet visited New York but the city has (in recent years) become the idea of a desired 'new' point of transition to a fuller and less cloistered life. Nevinson's emergence from the war into modernity and its symbol, New York, reminds me of the destructiveness of my earlier life and the compelling need to find hope in other countries. I travelled as far as the desert and the Atlas mountains in Northern Africa and to St. Petersburg and Novgorod in Russia. I have never, though, visited the United States, even though I have taught American students at The University of Notre Dame in London for many years. The reason I give for this has been that I do not fly, not because I am afraid of flying, but owing to a virus that affected my inner ear (viral labyrinthitis) and made me very dizzy over fifteen years ago. It took several years to recover my balance and I've been told by my doctor that the weight of air pressure in flying might possibly affect a weakened inner ear and bring on the dizziness again – it probably won't, though, he smiled. I have not yet dared put his uncertain diagnosis to the test.

Freud writes of 'the legend of the Labyrinth', recalling the story of the Cretan minotaur (half man half bull) living at the heart of a maze, whom Theseus, Ariadne's lover, slays. Theseus finds his way out of the maze with the aid of Ariadne's thread. He is led out of a dangerous womb into the world outside. Freud interprets the Labyrinth as 'a representation of anal birth: the twisting paths are the bowels and Ariadne's thread is the umbilical cord.' [120]

Viral labyrinthitis de-stablised and debilitated me for several years and in that time I was enabled to 'break' down and emerge from an illness which in many ways defined my 'anal' state of mind. I was a

---

[120] Freud, 'Revision of the Theory of Dreams', 25, XXII (1932 – 1936) ibid

daughter caught up in an intense love for both her 'Freudian' father and long-deceased brother. I cannot, would not wish to, map the myth in total onto my own family 'affair' but I can say that the 'thread' I held led me onto dark pathways and into a maze at the centre of which were some very angry and ugly feelings turned monstrous. I have discovered the 'monster' in myself who has held onto my own and my brother, Andrew's angry pain. He was the child in my mother's womb – there before me and whose place I had usurped. My relative 'normality' was envied bitterly by my brother and also by my angrier self.

Freud writes that the girl dreams of meeting her father, who was there before her in search of the mother's womb. Without wishing to speak for her, I think both my father and my brother, Andrew, have been 'first' in my mother's mind-womb, even though her hopes were in many ways (I think) transferred to me, the daughter who came after. Other stories eventually swam into view with the arrival of my nine years younger brother, Robert, and eleven years younger sister, Liz, and they have much to tell. They help me to see the bigger picture.

I am beginning to emerge into a life and a psyche that are independent of my male forebears.

One day I'll sail into New York harbour on a working boat from Scandinavia. Like Robert Louis Stevenson or the sailor for twenty years, Joseph Conrad, I shall sit and stand on deck in all weathers, simply watching the sea or held in its sway. One day I'll cross the Atlantic Ocean like one of those intrepid Victorians, Charles and Catherine Dickens among them, who in 1842 took the first steam-boat crossing to America. I will take my own 'breakfast-ship' to America.

In the last room of the exhibition I came upon a painting that arrested me for a good half an hour and I returned to the gallery to view Nevinson's *A Studio in Montparnasse* (1926) many times after that first sighting. This large painting was presented to the Tate by H.G. Wells in 1927 and the 'studio' depicted has become *my* studio and also the time machine Wells dreamt up.

The painting depicts a naked woman stroking a black cat. She has dark bobbed hair and is standing, looking down at the cat, who is sitting on a window seat gazing out at Montparnasse and its large apartment blocks. She is purring (I am purring – my hair too is dark and bobbed, but I am older and sixty years young) at a dome in the distance. At a guess the studio is on the third or fourth floor of one of those Parisian blocks. The window is huge and takes up most of one wall, its panes tall and narrow. The floor to ceiling curtains are heavy (maybe velvet) with a black background and a barely discernible red pattern of swirling lines. The curtains are drawn aside and secured loosely by gold and black tie-backs, as though the young woman had just got out of bed to let in the light. Her clothes are draped across a small chair, a green cloche hat perched on its back. She seems comfortable in her nakedness, as though she had only recently discovered the freedom of dispensing with clothes.

Nevinson's mother Margaret was one of seventy women who had broken away from the Women's Social and Political Union in 1907 to found the Women's Freedom League. By contrast with the WSPU the Freedom League opposed violence to attain political ends, specifically the suffrage. Margaret's son, Christopher, was also a pacifist and, before being appointed an Official war artist, he drove ambulances for the Red Cross on the front line like many conscientious objectors. I associate the Nevinsons with liberty, peacefulness and reparation.

A Studio in Montparnasse is a picture of relative calm, despite the fact that Sisley Huddleston, the writer who occupied this studio, went on to support Vichy France during the Second World War. Huddleston did in fact protest that Nevinson had introduced the figure of the naked woman who was not in the original sketch. I like the idea of the woman, this surprising new visitor, being a later addition and at her ease in the picture. The cat sits at the centre of the window and of the painting, the young woman's hand gently placed on her back. There is a sense that something may be about to happen.

To the left of the cat, its back to the window, there is a small pink sofa, upon which there are some casually scattered papers and an orange cushion. In front of the sofa there is a framed painting, set on an easel, of a large spindly figure in motion. It is hard to see the subject and then I notice that the wooden floor of the studio appears to be sloping down from the window, as if all the furniture were at a tilt and about to slide toward the viewer. A young couple viewing the picture with me also notice this and together we wonder what is going on.

The woman, the cat and the little chair are, though, stable elements in the picture. The couple move away, smiling at me before walking out of the exhibition toward the gallery shop, a busy hub of visitors. When my eye rests in the foreground of the picture I realise I'm looking down on the chair and the dining room table that stands on a green and red striped rug. There is a bowl of bananas and oranges, a small flowering plant and a few books scattered on the table.

This was one of Nevinson's works exhibited at the Leicester Galleries in March 1926, which had caught the eye of H.G. Wells, author and connoisseur of women, a champion of their equality and freedom. The back of the naked woman turned away from the viewer and toward the cat surely intrigued Wells, who was both woman's friend and her philanderer.

I like to think that this young woman, when she has finished enjoying her sensual moment in the clear light of day, will put on her clothes, not forgetting the green cloche hat with its small splash of red (a feather or a flower) and sit down on the chair by the window. There she will summon the energy and composure necessary for time-travelling. She will slither down the studio floor into futurity, knowing that everything will be in place (albeit at a tilt) on her return.

If she dawdles or hurries, there's a danger that the studio scene will lose its footing and the furniture slide away irretrievably in its tilt toward the viewer and the outside world. The artist and the viewer gaze from a height at this scene. I imagine a step-ladder outside the frame, upon which Nevinson is perched with his easel. He would have needed to take care not to fall, along with his paints, into the studio where his potentially overbearing presence may scatter the wits and composure of his imaginary model.

I return in half a minute to my real studio, my head and heart full of what I have viewed. After leaving my Surrey home at nineteen years old I occupied multiple bedsits and flats (twenty or so as far as I can recall). These places I never called home were mostly in London. I stayed a month in Paris in my early twenties, but I cannot remember where. I like to think it was Montparnasse on the left bank of the Seine. The memory is a blur of alcohol and sexual obsession.

I have never visited the Montparnasse Cemetery where Charles Baudelaire and Jean Paul Sartre and Simone de Beauvoir, along with Samuel Beckett, are buried. Beckett is the last in my list and the first writer I came to love when I lived in Dublin for a few years. I realise now that Beckett's humanity and humour were what I most cherished. I also registered the despair in his work way back then, without imagining how much his writing would continue to help me in my life. I can see now that 'happy days' (however sobering or absurd) are here, not elsewhere.

George Eliot (aka Marian Evans), a writer who dealt with complex and interwoven realities at multiple levels and in exquisite intricacy of detail, wrote in the epigraph to her last great novel, *Daniel Deronda*, that we 'can do nothing without the make-believe of a beginning'. At the beginning of my book I recounted my visit to a talk on Eliot's novel, *Middlemarch*, at The Institute of Psychoanalysis as the background of my discovery of Edwin Landseer's *The Arab Tent*. That day in 1992, over twenty years ago, was the beginning of my engagement with psychoanalysis and with paintings, the start of my journey into art and an exploration of the ways pictures have played on my mind.

Every time I step into the gallery nearby or further afield, each time I look at a painting (however long I've known it), I am in the process of make-believing a beginning again and that act (repeated daily, hourly, in every moment that passes) possesses its very own truth. Belief involves asserting one's claim on life. Eliot's 'make-believe of a beginning' keeps ringing true for me. To paint a picture or to write a book is a leap of faith that must begin with one's own particular and partial view, which is rooted in the experience of the small children we once were. My love of the paintings I have meditated in this book required me to believe both in the picture and in myself (as a child and as an adult). There is an element of 'make-believe' in everything we do, from the most mundane task to a deep study. Every day requires an act of courage as we rise from our beds to begin again and again, and pictures can help us. My father's twenty-four volumes of Freud have been my daily companions on this journey. They have helped me to 'make-believe' a life that is beginning to make sense.

I began with The Arab Tent and I end much closer to home with A Studio in Paris. My imagination has moved from Landseer's oriental animals to a woman with dark bobbed hair standing in a Montparnassian studio and looking from the window at a wider world. She possesses a room with a view of Paris, whilst my tall windows in this London village are filled with mature trees and the younger saplings that have grown in their shade. My therapists are at my side. A woman and a man are holding and letting me go both in the same breath. Soon, but not too soon, it might be time to say goodbye and step into that 'breakfast-ship' of Freud's poetic imagination. I will take it out of this book and into my life in the world.

The green and red striped rug in Nevinson's studio is not a magic carpet. The rug gives the studio a really good colour, as though he has introduced warmth and an idea of growth to the picture. I bought a new rug, striped red and amber and green, from John Lewis just before (or was it after?) seeing A Studio at Montparnasse. The rug is by my bed (become a boat) ensuring a safe landing when I step out of pictures and into the day.

SOURCES

David Boyd Haycock, Nash Nevinson Spencer Gertler Carrington Bomberg: A Crisis of Brilliance,
1908-1922, 2013

C.R. W. Nevinson, Paint and Prejudice, 1938

Afterword

My mother (Dinah Gregory) died very recently on October 7th 2014, five days before my father died on October 12th 1990. She did not suffer as the illness was sudden and swift. My siblings, Robert and Liz, Lucy (my niece) and I were at her side around the clock for six days and nights, and then early one morning she died. Robert (alone among women) stayed strong for us all. My sister slept in a little bed beside our mother's. I was on my own with her when she died. I was singing a cradle song to my mother, breathing in and out in time with her halting breath. I think she knew I was there, hoping her death might be painless, which it was. When my mother died I was in the middle of revising *The Studio* to send off to Alice, my editor, at Free Association Books. I read an extract at my mother's funeral and wished she might have been there. Friends and relations came from far and wide to remember and to celebrate my mother's long life. She was on the cusp of eighty-seven years old. My brother, sister, Lucy and I conducted the funeral service without a minister or humanist presiding. We did it ourselves and sang *All Things Bright and Beautiful* and *Lord of All Hopefulness*. We made speeches and gave readings, the service concluding with the glorious sounds of Ella Fitzgerald and Louis Armstrong singing and playing George Gershwin's *Summertime*. Afterwards we gathered at *The Yew Tree* in Reigate to talk and to cry and to laugh in memory of our dear mother. In the garden of the pub there is a small yew tree in a pot and it is growing rapidly. The owners could not see a mature yew tree when they bought the pub and they are hopeful that this little tree, once taken out of the pot and planted among mature trees, will fill out and become beautiful. I will return there, alone or with family and friends, to remember my mother. My brother, Robert, is standing on a chair. 'Can I have your attention everyone?' he smiles. And then he raises his glass and we all toast our mother in her heart-breaking absence. The service we made our own and *The Yew Tree* gathering were (I hope) very much in her style. I shall miss her so much. This book and its cargo are for her.

Appendix 1
The Stoop Bequest

The list of the paintings in Frank Stoop's bequest is online with the Tate and is also held in the Tate archive.   The details below are courtesy of the Tate.

Tate Collection: C Frank Stoop: List of Works

1. Georges Braque   *Bather (Baigneuse)*, 1925
2.   "   "   *Guitar & Jug (Guitare et pichet)*, 1927
3. Paul Cezanne   *Still Life with Water Jug (Nature morte a la cruche)*, circa 1892-3
4.   "   "   *The Gardener Vallier (Le Jardinier Vallier)*, circa 1906
5. Edgar Degas   *Bed-Time (Le Coucher)*, circa 1880-85
6.   "   "   *Woman at her Toilet (Femme a sa toilette)*, circa 1894
7. H. Gaudier-Brzeska *Head of a Child*, 1912-13
8.   "   "   *Head of a Girl*, circa 1912-13
9.   "   "   *Lion*, circa 1912-13
10.   "   "   *Leopard I*, circa 1912-13
11.   "   "   *Leopard II*, circa 1912-13
12.   "   "   *Jaguar*, circa 1912-13
13.   "   "   *Puma I*, circa 1912-13
14.   "   "   *Puma II*, circa 1912-13

15.   "   "   *Eland*, circa 1912-13

16.   "   "   *Verso: Traces of Sketch of Bison*, circa 1912-13

17.   "   "   *Studies of Birds*, circa 1912-13

18.   "   "   *Vulture I*, circa 1912-13

19.   "   "   *Vulture II*, circa 1912-13

20.   "   "   *Vulture III*, circa 1912-13

21.   "   "   *Vulture IV*, circa 1912-13

22.   "   "   *Singer*, 1913

23.   "   "   *Red Stone Dancer*, circa 1913

24.   "   "   *Man on a Horse*, 1913

25.   "   "   *Tiger*, 1913

26.   "   "   *The Imp*, circa 1914

27. Vincent Van Gogh   *Thatched Roofs*, 1884

28.   "   "   *A Corner of the Garden of St. Paul's Hospital at St Remy*, 1889

29.   "   "   *Farms near Auvers*, 1890

30.   "   "   *The Oise at Auvers*

31. Marie Laurencin   *Portraits (Marie Laurencin, Cecilia de Madrazo and the Dog Coco)* 1915

32. Henri Matisse   *Nude Study in Blue*, circa 1899-1900

33.   "   "   *Trivaux Pond*, 1916 or 1917

34. Amedeo Modigliani *Portrait of a Girl*, circa 1917

35. Pablo Picasso   *Girl in a Chemise*, circa 1905

36.   "   "   *Horse with a Youth in Blue*, 1905-6

37.   "   "   *Seated Woman in a Chemise*, 1923

38. Henri Rousseau   *Bouquet of Flowers*, circa 1909-10

39. Walter Sickert   *Miss Gwen Ffrangcon-Davies as Isabella of France*, 1932

Appendix 2

Dr. H.A.C. Gregory's cargo

i. Frontispiece from Sotheby's Catalogue of the paintings by John Constable my paternal grandfather, Dr. H.A.C. Gregory put up for sale. Courtesy of Sotheby's.

ii. Dedications on three opera scores Benjamin Britten gave to my grandfather.

iii. List of paintings by John Constable from my grandfather's collection, in Carlos Peacock's *The Aldeburgh Festival of Music & the Arts Programme Book,* June 5th – June 13th, 1948.

CATALOGUE

OF

THE WELL-KNOWN COLLECTION

OF

PAINTINGS AND DRAWINGS

BY JOHN CONSTABLE, R.A.

INCLUDING

THE RENOWNED "MARINE PARADE AND CHAIN PIER, BRIGHTON, "

PORTRAITS; OIL SKETCHES OF LANDSCAPES, CLOUDS, SEASCAPES ; WATER-COLOURS, PENCIL DRAWINGS, ETC.

ALSO

IMPORTANT WATER-COLOURS AND DRAWINGS

BY BONINGTON, GAINSBOROUGH AND GIRTIN

OIL PAINTINGS

BY COTMAN AND RICHARD WILSON

FINE MODERN PICTURES

BY SICKERT AND UTRILLO

The Property of Dr. H. A. C. Gregory, M.C.

WHICH WILL BE SOLD BY AUCTION

BY MESSRS.

SOTHEBY & CO.

C. G. DES GRAZ, C.B.E.   C. V. PILKINGTON.   P. C. WILSON.   J. C. BUTTERWICK.
A. R. A. HOBSON.   A. J. 'B. KIDDELL.   T. H. CLARKE, M.B.E.

Auctioneers of Literary Property and Works Illustrative of the Fine Arts

AT THEIR LARGE GALLERIES, 34 & 35, NEW BOND STREET, W.1

On WEDNESDAY, the 20th day of JULY, 1949

AT **ELEVEN** O'CLOCK PRECISELY

On View at least Four Days Previous (Not Saturdays)
Catalogues may be had

Illustrated Catalogue (15 Plates) Price 7/-

A **Printed List of all Prices and Buyers' Names at this sale can be supplied for two shillings, and for all sales at low subscription rates.**

(i)

(ii)

Peter Grimes, with handwritten dedication, 'For Dr. Gregory with best wishes Benjamin Britten – alas, no Constable but the best I can do!' Sadler's Wells, 7th June 1945.

The Rape of Lucretia, 'To Dr. Gregory with every good wish, Benjamin Britten' Glyndebourne, 12th – 27th July, 1946.

Albert Herring, 'For Dr. Gregory with my best wishes and thanks for his great help for the first Aldeburgh Festival, Benjamin Britten, May 1948' Glyndebourne, 20th June 1947.

SANDHILLS and PRIOR'S HILL

JOHN CONSTABLE, R.A.
(1776 - 1837)

AN EXHIBITION OF OIL PAINTINGS, WATER COLOURS AND DRAWINGS FROM THE COLLECTION OF DOCTOR H. A. C. GREGORY, M.C.

OIL PAINTINGS

1. Cornfield near Brighton
2. Trees and Meadows
3. Landscape with Group of Trees
4. Landscape with River Estuary
5. Study of Elder Trees
6. Seascape with figure of a Seaman at the water's edge
7. Seascape with a beached Boat, and Shipping in the distance
8. Seascape with breaking Waves under a dark Sky
9. Sky study: white Clouds in a blue Sky
10. Sky study: blue and white Cloud effects
11. Sky study: blue and pink Sky with Spires or Tree Stems silhouetted against it
12. Sky study above Landscape and Trees
13. Sky study above Tree Tops
14. Sky study above a brownish Headland
15. Interior of Stable
16. Portrait

WATER COLOURS AND DRAWINGS

A separate list of these will be available at the Exhibition.

(iii)

List of paintings my grandfather, Dr. H.A.C. Gregory, exhibited at the first Aldeburgh Festival in 1948.

In a Note to the Exhibition Carlos Peacock writes: 'His [Constable's] was the farmer's eye that by long training can take in at a glance all the signs and portents of the land. It is perhaps significant that Dr. Gregory, the owner of this fine collection of Constable pictures, is himself a farmer whose work in connection with the breeding of Ayrshire cattle has won him international fame. From the many Constable paintings and drawings in his possession this comprehensive exhibition has been assembled.' Carlos Peacock.

List of paintings discussed in *The Studio*

Paul Cezanne, *The Gardener Vallier*, c. 1906, Tate Britain; *Portrait of a Peasant*, 1905-6, Museo Thyssen-Bornemisza; *Still Life with Water Jug*, c 1892-83, National Gallery (London) on loan from Tate Britain

John Constable, *The Marine Parade and Old Chain Pier, Brighton*, 1827, Tate Britain

Henri Gaudier-Brzeska, *Red Stone Dancer*, c 1913, Tate Britain; *Bison; Eland; Jaguar; Leopards I & II; Lion; Pumas I & II; Studies of Birds; Tiger; Vultures I,II,III,IV*, 1912-13, Tate Britain

Edwin Landseer, *The Arab Tent*, 1866, The Wallace Collection

John Frederick Lewis, *Study of the Courtyard of the Coptic Patriarch's House in Cairo*, c 1864, Tate Britain

C.R.W. Nevinson, *A Studio in Montparnasse*, 1926, Tate Britain; *Temples of New York*, 1919, Victoria & Albert Museum; *The Viaduct at Issy-les-Moulineaux*, 1913, Collection Robyn & Mitchel Martin-Weber, Sydney, Australia; *Le Vieux Port*, 1913-14, The Government Art Collection, UK

Painter unknown (initials RG), *The Zebra*, c 1790-1830, Private Collection

George Stubbs, *Zebra*, 1762-63, Yale Center for British Art, Paul Mellon Collection

Vincent Van Gogh, *Sunflowers*, 1888, National Gallery (London); *Thatched Roofs*, 1884, Tate Britain; *A Corner of the Garden of St. Paul's Hospital at St. Remy*, 1889, Tate Britain; *Farms near Auvers*, 1890, Tate Britain; *The Oise at Auvers*, 1890, Tate Britain

Bibliography

Isobel Armstrong, *Language As Living Form in 19ᵗʰ-Century Poetry*, 1982

Enid Bagnold, *Autobiography*, 1917

Martin Bailey, *The Sunflowers Are Mine*, 2013

Elizabeth Barrett Browning, *Sonnets from the Portuguese*, 1844

Samuel Beckett, *Waiting for Godot*, 1953-55; *Happy Days*, 1961

Ulrike Becks-Malorny, *Paul Cezanne: Pioneer of Modernism*, 2006

John Berger, *Here Is Where We Meet: A Story of Crossing Paths*, 2006

Charlotte Bronte, *Jane Eyre*, 1847

Robert Browning, *Men & Women*, 1855

Antonia Byatt, *Portraits in Fiction*, 2001

Lewis Carroll, *Alice's Adventures in Wonderland*, 1865

Tony Currie, *The Radio Times Story*, 2001

H.S. Ede, *Savage Messiah*, 1971

George Eliot, *Middlemarch*, 1871-72; *Daniel Deronda*, 1876

Sandra Evans, *Talking Over The Years*, 2004

E.M. Forster, 'The Machine Stops', *Collected Short Stories*, 1972

Sigmund Freud, *The Standard Edition of the Complete Psychological Works of Sigmund Freud*, translated from the German under the General Editorship of James Strachey, The Hogarth Press & The Institute of Psychoanalysis, London, 1953

David Boyd Haycock, *A Crisis of Brilliance, 1908-22*, 2013

Susan Hogan, *Healing Arts: The History of Art Therapy*, 2001

Edmund D Jones (ed), *English Critical Essays on 19th century poetry*, 1916/1968

C.S. Lewis, *The Lion, the Witch & the Wardrobe*, 1950

Michael Lewis, *J.F. Lewis*, 1978

C.R.W. Nevinson, *Paint & Prejudice*, 1938

Anne Robbins *An essay by Ann Dumas, Cezanne in Britain*, National Gallery, 2006

Gillian Rose, *Love's Work: A Reckoning with Life*, 1995

Frances Spalding, *The Tate: A History*, 1998

Adrian Stokes (Introduction & Notes), *Cezanne*, The Faber Gallery, 1947

W.M. Thackeray, *Notes on a journey from Cornhill to grand Cairo: by way of Lisbon, Athens, Constantinople, and Jerusalem, performed in the steamers of the Peninsular & Oriental Company*, by M.A. Titmarsh [pseudonym], 1846

H.G. Wells, *The Time Machine*, 1895

Simon Wilson, *Tate Gallery: An Illustrated Companion*, Tate Gallery, 1991

D.W. Winnicott, *The Child, The Family & The Outside World*, 1964

Virginia Woolf, *Walter Sickert: a conversation*, The Hogarth Press (1934), 2005

William Wordsworth, *The Prelude*, 1850

Emile Zola, *L'Oeuvre*, 1886

My father, Dr. B.A.J.C. Gregory's papers are held (holding P42) in the archive at The Institute of Psychoanalysis, Byron House, 112A, Shirland Road, London W9 2BT. For information about the archive contact Mrs. Joanne Halford, Archivist, archives@iopa.org.uk

Index